DOWN TRODDEN

James Massey

DOWN
TRODDEN

The Struggle of India's Dalits
for Identity, Solidarity
and Liberation

Risk
BOOK SERIES

WCC Publications, Geneva

Cover design: Edwin Hassink

Cover photo: WCC/Gerhard Thiel

IBSN 2-8254-1230-9

© 1997 WCC Publications, World Council of Churches,
150 route de Ferney, 1211 Geneva 2, Switzerland

No. 79 in the Risk Book Series

Printed in Switzerland

Table of Contents

Introduction

The involvement of the World Council of Churches with the Dalits of India goes back to a key moment in the WCC's history. During the 1970s, the Council determined to go beyond the traditional ecumenical role of denouncing racism as incompatible with the gospel of Jesus Christ and take a prophetic stance through actions of solidarity with racially oppressed groups. The risks in this approach became evident in the controversy that arose over grants from the Council's Special Fund to Combat Racism to the Patriotic Front in Zimbabwe, which was engaged in an armed struggle to overturn white minority rule there.

The vigorous debate in its member churches led the WCC in 1980 to convene a consultation in the Netherlands on the future of the ecumenical struggle against racism. During this consultation a lone voice from India raised the plight of Indian Dalits. In her account of this consultation (*Race: No Peace without Justice*, Geneva, WCC Publications, 1980), Barbara Rogers recalls this poignant moment:

> A representative of the Untouchables [Dalits] caused quite a stir when he called for the floor microphone at the end of one long session to plead for outside help for his people. He broke down in tears as he told the plenary that Untouchables were being murdered, beaten, raped and abused every day throughout India, while nobody outside knew what was happening and the people were completely friendless within India itself... Many were very moved by his appeal and the very evident despair it conveyed (p.31).

Speaking of this episode later, WCC general secretary Konrad Raiser suggested that "the consultation did not know how to handle it, because it was not yet an organized struggle; it was just a cry. But it was a cry that was difficult to bypass."

Three years later, during the WCC's sixth assembly in Vancouver, Bishop M. Azariah (then general secretary of the Church of South India, now the bishop of Madras) made a forceful plea to include the issue of the Dalits in what the assembly said about human rights. Although that plea was not successful, over the next eight years the Dalit struggle in

India – and the participation in it of Dalit Christians – intensified; and the solitary voices heard in WCC circles in 1980 and 1983 became a collective cry.

At the seventh assembly of the WCC, held in Canberra in 1991, the cry of the Dalits was clearly heard by the world church. The assembly responded by including in its statement on indigenous people the following words: "We affirm the growing consciousness of the indigenous peoples' struggles for freedom, including that of the Dalits of India." Following this mandate from the assembly, Bob Scott of the Council's programme unit on Justice, Peace and Creation contacted Dalit activists in both North and South India. The animator's role which he played eventually resulted in the formation of the interfaith Dalit Solidarity Programme (DSP), described in greater detail in chapter 3 of this book.

During his 1995 visit to India, Konrad Raiser addressed the members of the National Working Committee of the DSP. Acknowledging the depth and special features of Dalit oppression, he assured them of the WCC's continuing commitment to the Dalit issue:

> I want in particular to express our specific commitment to approaching the Dalit issue in an interfaith way, bringing together in a relationship of solidarity Dalit leaders from Buddhist, Sikh, Muslim, Hindu and Christian backgrounds. We feel this is all the more important in a situation where religious loyalties have so often been misused in order to mobilize intercommunal conflict and hatred. In such a situation the DSP, organized on an interfaith basis, has a chance of making a witness that could become of significance far beyond the immediate circle of concerns of the Dalit community.

By bringing out this short book as part of the WCC Publications Risk Book Series, the Council is offering a further indication of its commitment to the cause of the Dalits in India. I would like to express my thanks and appreciation to the WCC Publications staff for publishing a book which will, I hope, contribute not only to internationalizing the Dalit issue but also to encouraging support for the cause of the Dalits through the ecumenical movement.

This volume is perhaps the first major work on the Dalit issue published outside India in English and addressed to an international as well as an Indian readership. In these chapters I have sought to take the Dalit issue as a whole, seeing Dalit Christians as part of the total Dalit community, which includes persons of different faiths and ideologies. The first three chapters – on "terminology", "history" and "struggle" – thus unfold the concerns of all the Dalits in India. Despite their more specific Christian focus, chapters four and five – on "theology" and "church" – must also be read while keeping in mind the entire Dalit community. And the vision of "liberation" developed in the final chapter should be taken as one which presents a future hope for the entire Dalit community, but also for the whole global human community. In this last chapter, one will find echoes of the experiences and visions of other oppressed communities, drawing in particular on what the late Paulo Freire described in his classic work on the *Pedagogy of the Oppressed*. This aspect of the liberation of the Dalits also places these issues in a global context.

I conclude these introductory words by offering this short volume to all who would like to join in "re-creating a new human being, who will neither be the oppressor nor the oppressed – who on the contrary will be a 'person in the process of liberation'".

Delhi, October 1997   *James Massey*

1. Terminology

The term "dalit" is derived from the Sanskrit root *dal*, which means burst, split, broken or torn asunder, downtrodden, scattered, crushed, destroyed. But although the term has ancient roots, its contemporary usage to specify a section of the people of India who have suffered oppression throughout history under the prevailing religious and social norms goes back only a few decades. As such *dalit* has become part of the vocabulary of all the North Indian languages. For example, the well-known Hindi dictionary *Bhasa-Sabad Kos* describes *dalit* as "an undeveloped or backward section of people, such as among the Hindu untouchables (*achut*) or serving caste (*shudra*)". In Panjabi, the *Mahan Kos* of Bhai Kahan Singh defines *dalit* as one who belongs to the lowest caste (*hini jati*) and has been trampled down by or broken under the feet of the upper caste (*uchi jatan*).

The seeds of this understanding of *dalit* lie in the writings of two great Indian personalities: the 19th-century reformer and revolutionary Mahatma Jyotiba Phule, and the 20th-century intellectual and revolutionary B.D. Ambedkar. Mahatma Phule used the terminology *shudra-atishudra* for Dalits. *Shudras* are "touchable backward castes" and *atishudras* are "untouchable backward castes". In order to enslave the *shudras* and *atishudras*, Mahatma Phule said, the *brahmin* or priestly caste conspired to divide them into these two classes. Ambedkar wrote in detail about *shudras* and untouchables in two well-known works, *Who Were the Shudras?* (1947) and *The Untouchables* (1948). In his writings, he used the English term "untouchable" (*achuta*) for "dalit".

The recent use of the term "dalit" has been developed in the manifesto of the Dalit Panther Movement of the Indian state of Maharashtra, published in Bombay in 1973. Responding to the question "Who is a Dalit?", this manifesto says: "members of scheduled castes and tribes, neo-Buddhists, the working people, the landless and poor peasants, women and all those who are being exploited politically, economically and in the name of religion".

It is this sense of the term which is used in this book. The Dalit people are those who, on the basis of caste distinctions, have been considered "outcastes", because the architects of the system did not see fit to include them in the graded four-fold caste structure of Indian society. On the basis of this status they have been made to bear extreme forms of disadvantage and oppression for centuries, a continuous assault on their humanity which virtually reduced them to a state of being "no-people".

The Dalit Panther Movement manifesto makes clear the broader concerns of the movement:

> We must pay attention to the objective process of social development and make an historical analysis of the power that imprisons the Dalit and which has succeeded in making him tie his own hands. The Hindu feudal rule can be a hundred times more ruthless today in oppressing the Dalits than it was in the Muslim period or the British period, because the Hindu feudal rule has in its hands all the arteries of production, bureaucracy, judiciary, army and police forces, in the shape of feudals, landlords, capitalists and religious leaders who stand behind and enable these instruments to thrive. Hence the problem of untouchability of the Dalits is no more of mere mental slavery. Untouchability is the most violent form of exploitation on the face of the earth, which survives the ever-changing forms of the power structure. Today it is necessary to seek its origin, its root causes. If we understand them, we can definitely strike at the heart of this exploitation... Truly speaking, the problem of the Dalits, or Scheduled Castes and Tribes, has become a broad problem; the Dalit is no longer merely an untouchable outside the village walls and the scripture. He is not only an untouchable, and a Dalit, but he is also a worker, a landless labourer, a proletarian.

A variety of other names have been used in both English and Indian languages to designate these people who are outside the social structure because of the contempt and hatred shown by others. Besides the terms "scheduled castes" and "untouchables", the terms "exterior castes", "depressed classes" and *harijan* have become well-known and will be used at several points in the historical account in this book. What is most important to emphasize at this point is that "Dalit" is the term these downtrodden people have given to themselves. This helps to account for the popularity of the term among Dalit people of different protest movements in India. "Dalit" is thus not a mere descriptive name or title, but an expression of hope for the recovery of their past identity. The struggle of these "outcastes" has given the term *dalit* a positive meaning. The very realization of themselves as Dalit, the very acceptance of the state of "dalitness", is the first step on the way towards their transformation into full and liberated human beings.

The Bible and the Dalits

In his Hindi translation of the New Testament in the early 1960s Yesu Das Tewari used the term *dalit* to render the Greek word *tethrausmenoi* ("oppressed" or "downtrodden") in Luke's account (4:18-19) of the sermon at the synagogue in Nazareth in which Jesus proclaimed the "year of the Lord's favour" and declared his own jubilee ministry of bringing good news to the poor (*din jano*), release to the captives (*bandio*), recovery of sight to the blind (*andon*) and liberation to the oppressed (*dalito*). Subsequent Hindi translators of the New Testament have followed this lead, which has helped to popularize the term among Christian groups who are fighting for the rights of the Dalits.

An intriguing connection has also been drawn between the Sanskrit root *dal*, which we mentioned earlier, and the Hebrew root *dal*, whose meaning is to hang down, to be languid, weakened, low and feeble. Because Sanskrit and Hebrew belong to two different linguistic families – the Indo-Germanic and the Semitic – some scholars would describe the linguistic connection between the two roots as mere coincidence. Be that as it may, a reading of some of the fifty or so passages in which the Hebrew root *dal* appears in the biblical literature can shed some fascinating light on the situation of Dalits in India today. The fact that Indian biblical scholars, translators and interpreters have not previously taken note of the parallel between what the Old Testament is talking about and the workings of the caste system can be explained by the contextual nature of all biblical interpretation. The training of these Indian scholars has been European, particularly British; and whatever concern they have shown for relating the biblical message to the Indian context has largely been limited to what are considered the great world religions of India. For the most part they have ignored the context of the masses of Indian people, which the Dalit concern addresses.

While *dal* in the Old Testament is often understood as "poor" merely in terms of the economic status of certain people, some interpreters have gone beyond this in an attempt to understand the situation more deeply. For example, in an essay on the term "poor" in *The Interpreter's Dictionary of the Bible*, C.U. Wolf writes:

> They are those whose prosperity and social status have been reduced. In this respect they are the opposite of the rich (Exodus 23:3; 30:15; Leviticus 14:21; Proverbs 22:16). In physical strength, in psychological ability, they are also impaired and helpless (Job 34:28; Psalm 82:3; Jeremiah 40:7; 52:16).

The important point made here by Wolf can also be applied to the situation of Dalits in India. That is, the *dal* are not only economically and physically poor or weak, but they are poor in their "psychological ability"; indeed, their being has been "impaired" to such an extent that they have become "helpless".

If we turn now to some of the texts themselves, we may perhaps deepen our understanding of both the biblical context and its application to the situation in India. We shall divide this brief selection into four points, citing a number of texts in each case (using the English of the New Revised Standard Version and italicizing the word used to translate the root *dal*).

1. The existence of "Dalits" was part and parcel of the life of the people of the Old Testament.

Both the presence of and the concern for the Dalits were not merely abstract matters of sociological or economic fact, but part of the total reality of life which one encounters every day. Exodus 30:15 provides that "the rich shall not give more, and *the poor* shall not give less, than the half-shekel, when you bring this offering to the Lord to make atonement for your lives". In the long speech with which he concludes his defence of himself, Job says: "If I have withheld anything that *the poor* desired, or have caused the eyes of the widow to fall..., then let my shoulder blade fall from my shoulder, and let my arm be broken from its socket" (Job 31:16-22). And Psalm 82, a plea for justice attributed to Asaph, urges: "Give justice to *the weak* and the orphan; maintain the right of the lowly and the destitute. Rescue *the weak* and the needy; deliver them from the hand of the wicked" (vv.3-4).

2. As part of everyday life, the reality of dal has different shades of meaning.

A literal, descriptive sense of the word is found in Genesis 41:19, where Pharaoh tells Joseph of his dream, which foretold famine in Egypt: "Then seven other cows came up..., *poor*, very ugly and thin. Never had I seen such ugly ones in all the land of Egypt." The word can also describe someone's physical appearance. For example, in the horrifying story of the rape by David's son Amnon of his half-sister Tamar (2 Samuel 13), the scheming Jonadab plants the idea of how to attack Tamar by asking the lovesick Amnon, "O son of the king, why are you so *haggard* morning after morning?" (v.4). The book of Ruth uses the term in the economic sense, when Boaz says to Ruth, who has sought his protection, "May you be blessed by the Lord, my daughter...; you have not gone after young men, whether *poor* or rich" (3:10).

A political connotation of the term is evident in 2 Samuel 3:1: "There was a long war between the house of Saul and the house of David; David grew stronger and stronger, while the house of Saul became *weaker and weaker*." In other passages, one finds an even stronger link between the status of the poor and political power. Proverbs 28:3 says that "a ruler who oppresses *the poor* is a beating rain that leaves no food"; verse 15 of the same chapter adds: "like a roaring lion or a charging bear is a wicked ruler over *a poor people*". More positively, Proverbs 29:14 links the qualification of a good ruler with the justice he renders to the "Dalits": "If a king judges *the poor* with equity, his throne will be established forever."

Finally, there are some passages that establish a direct relationship between God and the Dalits. Isaiah's song of praise to the wonderful works of the Lord (ch. 25) includes these words: "You have been a refuge to *the poor*, a refuge to the needy in their distress, a shelter from the rainstorm and a shade from the heat" (v.4). A similar theme is found in one of the psalms of David, which begins, "Happy are those who consider *the poor*; the Lord delivers them in the day of trouble" (Ps. 41:1).

3. The existence of "Dalits" is the consequence of forces and processes in society which have affected certain people.

Several of the Old Testament passages which go into the question of how people become "Dalits" take the form of tragic laments sung on their behalf:

> They will give back the fruit of their toil,
> and will not swallow it down;
> from the profit of their trading they will get no enjoyment.
> For they have crushed and abandoned *the poor*;
> they have seized a house that they did not build.
>
> (Job 20:18f.)

> Do not remember against us the iniquities of our ancestors;
> let your compassion come speedily to meet us,
> for we are *brought very low*.
>
> (Psalm 79:8)

> Those who oppress *the poor*
> insult their Maker,
> but those who are kind to the needy
> honour him.
>
> (Proverbs 14:31)

> O Lord, do your eyes not look for truth?
> You have struck them,
> but they feel no anguish;
> you have consumed them,

but they have refused to take correction.
They have made their faces harder than rock;
they have refused to turn back.
Then I said, "These are only *the poor*,
they have no sense;
for they do not know the way of the Lord,
the law of their God."

(Jeremiah 5:3-4)

Here we have cited a few of the passages in the Old Testament in which the term *dal* is used for a section of the people of God. Many other incidents and stories in the Bible disclose the process by which certain people have been reduced to a state of "dalitness". Perhaps the earliest direct biblical reference to the idea that certain occupations are lower than others – and thus to the evil of untouchability – is found in Genesis 46:34, where Joseph tells his brothers that all shepherds are abhorrent to the Egyptians. Subsequently, the account beginning in Exodus 1:8 records how the Egyptians tried to turn this shepherd community into a community of nonentities by forcing on them "every kind of field labour" (Ex. 1:13).

Later, when under Moses' leadership God liberated this untouchable shepherd community, they in turn treated other communities more ruthlessly, reducing them to a state of "dalitness". A number of Old Testament stories illustrate this. For example, the book of Joshua tells how the Gibeonites were forced to become "hewers of wood and drawers of water" for the Israelites (9:27). The book of Judges illustrates more prevalent means of reducing defeated people: communities such as the Canaanites and the Amorites were obliged to do forced labour for the Israelites (cf. Judg. 1:28,30,35).

The passages cited above further testify to the ongoing oppression against "Dalits". The verses from Job 20 are part of a longer narrative in which Zophar, one of Job's friends, makes some observations about the wickedness of the powerful oppressors and their methods of oppressing others, including the poor (*dalim*). Verse 19 makes special reference to the oppression which the Dalits must submit to: they are left alone after being crushed, and even their houses are taken over by the oppressors.

The prophet Amos names these oppressors more explicitly. Denouncing the wealthy people of Israel, he says that they "trample the head of *the poor* into the dust of the earth" (2:7). Even rich women play the role of oppressors against the *dalim* (4:1). The prophet speaks to them in scathing terms on behalf of the Dalits:

> Hear this, you that trample on the needy,
>   and bring to ruin the poor (*ani*) of the land,
> saying, "When the new moon be over, so that we may sell grain;
>   and the sabbath, so that we may offer wheat for sale?
> We will make the ephah small and the shekel great,
>   and practise deceit with false balances,
> buying *the poor* for silver
>   and the needy for a pair of sandals,
> and selling the sweepings of wheat."
>
> (Amos 8:4-6)

How low a level the Dalits had reached in Amos's day is evident from this passage: one could even buy and sell them like commodities, for a few silver coins.

In the second passage quoted earlier, the Psalmist addresses his whole community as Dalit. This is like saying, "The whole of the Indian Christian community is composed of Dalits" – a point to which we shall return in greater detail in a subsequent chapter. Of course the Psalmist says that his community's sinking to this low estate is a result of the past collective sins of their ancestors. In the passage from Proverbs 14, the author identifies God the Creator with the treatment of the Dalits: to oppress the community of the *dal*, he says, is tantamount to oppressing and insulting God himself.

Perhaps the most poignant reality of "dalitness" is evident in the final passage quoted above from Jeremiah: the difficulty of changing their state. One may even beat them, but they feel no pain. So unconsciously have they accepted their

Dalit state that there is almost no way for them to be restored: this is the bitter truth in Jeremiah's words, "these are only *dalim*, they have no sense". To what extent is this the case with the majority of Dalits in India today?

4. Some passages link the present plight of the Dalits with a messianic message of hope.

Finally, we may look at a few texts which may be said to contain a "messianic" message because they point to a future liberation for the Dalits.

> But if he is *poor* and cannot afford so much, he shall take one male lamb for a guilt offering to be elevated, to make atonement on his behalf, and one-tenth of an ephah of choice flour mixed with oil for a grain offering and a log of oil; also two turtle-doves or two pigeons, such as he can afford, one for sin offering and the other for a burnt offering (Leviticus 14:21f.; see also Lev. 5:7; 12:8; Luke 2:22-24).

> A shoot shall come out from the stump of Jesse,
>   and a branch shall grow out of his roots.
> The spirit of the Lord shall rest on him...
> His delight shall be in the fear of the Lord.
> He shall not judge by what his eyes see,
>   or decide by what his ears hear;
> but with righteousness he shall judge *the poor*,
>   and decide with equity for the meek of the earth;
> he shall strike the earth with the rod of his mouth,
>   and with the breath of his lips he shall kill the wicked.
> Righteousness shall be the belt around his waist,
>   and faithfulness the belt around his loins.
>
>   (Isaiah 11:1-5)

> On that day you shall not be put to shame
>   because of all the deeds by which you have rebelled
>   against me;
> for then I will remove from your midst
>   your proudly exultant ones,
> and you shall no longer be haughty
>   in my holy mountain.
> For I will leave in the midst of you
>   a people humble and *lowly*.
> They shall seek refuge in the name of the Lord.
>   (Zephaniah 3:11-12)

The passage from Leviticus refers to an offering which was to be made as a sign of recovery or cleanliness by a person who had suffered leprosy. According to the Mosaic law, such a person was considered as unclean or "untouchable"; the word used in Hebrew for such a person in Leviticus 14:21 is *dal*. Reading these verses from Leviticus 14 alongside Leviticus 5:7 and 12:8, we find that a poor person who has committed a sin but cannot offer a standard offering for it may also bring "two turtle doves or two pigeons" (5:7). The same is also the case for a poor woman who is considered unclean or untouchable for a certain period after bearing a child. If she cannot afford a standard offering for her purification, she may also offer two turtle doves or two pigeons (12:8). Thus an ordinary poor person, a poor woman after childbirth and a person afflicted with leprosy are all considered on the same level – and these are all *dal*. From the passage in Luke 2 we learn that Mary the mother of Jesus offered two turtle doves for her purification after the birth of Jesus. This offering of Mary brings her Son closer to complete solidarity with the Dalits of this world.

The second passage cited above, from Isaiah 11, is one of the prophecies which has been taken to refer to the coming of the Messiah, fulfilled in Jesus Christ (cf. Acts 13:22f.; Rom. 15:7-13). St Paul says in Romans 15:12 that this "root of Jesse" will enable people who are considered "Gentiles" or "pagan" (those who are outside the chosen race) to glorify God, and he will rule over them as well. Isaiah 11 gives a summary of the divine kingdom of the future on this earth. The one who rules this divine kingdom will be the just ruler, who will not judge by what he sees or hears, but will judge the *dalim* with righteousness. The point is that from the beginning God's plan for the liberation of human beings included especially the liberation of Dalits.

In the third passage, quoted from the prophet Zephaniah, the prophet hints at the entire liberation of the Dalits. In that final liberated state, the meaning of the term *dalit* will change. Its negative connotation will turn into a positive one. Believers and true followers of God will be known as *ani wa-*

dal (humble and lowly). So, according to the prophet Zephaniah, a time will come when not only people who consider
themselves in our context as *dalit* will be wholly liberated,
but even the term *dalit* itself will be "liberated" and given
new meaning.

2. History

The situation of the Dalits in India today has its roots almost 3500 years ago, when the "first nation", the people settled in India from time immemorial, were invaded and defeated by the first colonizers, the Aryans. Their defeat has been recorded in the earliest Indian written document, the *Rigveda*. But what the *Rigveda* records is in fact only the beginning of a long story of oppression and exploitation of the Dalits, a story which has unfolded through the long history of India. Each of the four layers of colonization – by the Aryans, the Muslims, the British and the dominant powers in independent India – has added to and deepened the problem of Dalitness. In this chapter, we shall look successively at some major features of each of these stages.

Aryan colonization

The military subjugation of the "first nation" of India by the Aryan colonizers, as recorded in the *Rigveda*, tells only part of the story. For what has forced the Dalits into their present state was not only their physical defeat at the hands of a superior military force. Their opponents used many other methods, both religious and psychological, to enslave them: creation of religious myths, manipulation, divide and rule, policies of accommodation. Systematically, the first colonizers took away the basic human rights of the first people of India and managed to convince them that their resulting status had been ordained by God himself.

For example, according to the famous *Purusasukta* hymn in the *Rigveda*, the four castes were created by God from the four parts of his own body: "The *Brahmin* [priestly class] was his mouth, both his arms were the *Rajanya* [or *Ksatriya*, the warriors]. His thighs became the *Vaishya* [traders]; from his feet the *Sudra* [serving caste] was produced." On the basis of this hymn, Orthodox Hindus believe that the four-fold division of Indian society exists from the earliest times. All those human beings who did not fit into this fourfold structure were outcastes – outside the purview of the "divine body".

The text of the *Rigveda* took written form around 1000 B.C.E. This was followed by the Upanishadic vedic period, from around 800 B.C.E. until the end of the 6th century B.C.E. Certain references in the *Upanishads* attest to the deepening of the problems of the Dalits by the time these texts came into existence. For example, the *Chandogya Upanishad* not only refers to the three upper castes, but also compares a *Chandala* (outcaste) to a dog or a swine:

> Accordingly, those who are of pleasant conduct here – the prospect is, indeed, that they will enter a pleasant womb, either the womb of a *Brahmin*, or the womb of a *Ksatriya*, or the womb of a *Vaishya*. But those who are of stinking conduct here – the prospect is, indeed, that they will enter a stinking womb, either the womb of a dog, or the womb of a swine or the womb of a *chandala* (10:7).

This verse makes clear how the caste system functioned to further the degradation of the Dalits: the "womb" of an upper caste woman is described as "pleasant", whereas that of an outcaste is said to be a "stinking" one. It also indicates that one's caste status was seen as determined by one's conduct in a previous incarnation; that is, the notion of caste by birth was fully established.

The two great epics, the *Ramayana* and the *Mahabharata*, composed during the period between 600 B.C.E. and 500 C.E., describe the further deterioration of the Dalits' condition. Indeed, a story from the *Ramayana* shows how even the *Sudras* had become degraded. In Lord Rama's time only the three upper castes were allowed to do *tapasya* (penance and meditation). When one *Sudra* by the name of Samvuka nevertheless undertook penance in order to attain divinity, a 15-year-old Brahmin boy died as a result. The bereaved father complained to Lord Rama who, after learning the circumstances of the death, went in search of the *Sudra*. On meeting him, he said:

> "You are indeed blessed. Tell me, in which caste have you been born? I am Rama, son of Dasaratha. Out of curiosity I have asked you this question. Tell me the truth. Are you a *Brahmin*,

Ksatriya or a *Sudra*?" The ascetic replied, "O King! I am born of the *Sudra* caste. I want to attain divinity by such penance. Because I want to attain divinity, I will not tell lies. I am a *Sudra* by caste, and my name is Samvuka."

As soon as the ascetic uttered those words, Lord Rama drew his sword and severed Samvuka's head. When he then asked the gods to restore the *Brahmin* boy to life, he was told that he had already been revived the moment the *Sudra* ascetic was killed.

A story in the *Mahabharata* also illustrates the degraded state of the Dalits. Ekalavya, an indigenous boy, had to have his right thumb cut off because he had learned archery so well that his skill equalled that of Arjuna. The point is that the low castes and the Dalits were denied the right to education.

The *Bhagavad Gita* establishes the belief in the four castes by insisting that these were created by the Lord Krishna himself. It advises members of each caste to follow faithfully the duties prescribed for them on the basis of their caste (or, in the case of Dalits, their status as outcastes). That, says the *Bhagavad Gita*, is the way to salvation.

Another literary source which sheds light on the down-trodden state of the Dalits is the Ordinances of Manu, the *Manusmriti*. Composed during the first seven centuries C.E., these texts removed even the human identity of the Dalits, whose existence at least had been recognized up to that point. The *Manusmriti* accepts only the three "twice-born" castes – *Brahman*, *Ksatriya* and *Vaisya* – and the "once-born" *Sudras*. "There is no fifth [caste]." To explain the existence of those who were not of the four castes, *Manusmriti* put forward the concept of "mixed castes", which included those born from intercaste marriages: the so-called *anuloma* (upper caste man, lower caste woman) and *pratiloma* (lower caste man, upper caste woman). According to this principle, the offspring of *pratiloma* were considered the most degraded.

According to the *Manusmriti*, the most despised groups were *Chandala* (offspring of a *Sudra* man and a *Brahmin* woman) and *Sapaka* (offspring of a *Chandala* male and a *Pukkasa* female). Their fate was a cruel one:

> The dwelling of *Chandalas* and *Cavpacas* (*sapaka*) should be outside the village; they should be deprived of dishes; their property [consists of] dogs and asses. Their clothes [should be] the garments of the dead; and their ornaments [should be] broken dishes; and they must constantly wander about (*Manusmriti*, 10.51f.).

The *Chandalas* and *Sapakas* are supposed to be the forebears of today's Dalits.

Thus it is clear that by the time that the composition of the *Manusmriti* was complete, the status of the Dalits had reached its nadir. Aryan colonization had become complete. During this period of Aryan colonization, two religious protest movements – Jainism and Buddhism – came into existence, led by two *Ksatriya* princes, Mahavora (580-468 B.C.E.) and Gautama Buddha (563-483). To these figures we shall return later.

The Muslim period

We have seen that the plight of the Dalits was mainly rooted in the religious beliefs of the so-called upper-caste Aryans, which took their more or less final form as Hindu law (*Manusmriti*) around 700 C.E. By that time the Dalits' status had been reduced to the level of the non-human or even the non-existent.

Over the next thirteen centuries, with the three phases of colonization that we have identified, one might have expected that there would be an improvement in the status of the Dalits. After all, the colonizers during the first two of these phases belonged to religions (Islam and Christianity) whose teachings are based on strongly egalitarian principles; and post-independence India is constitutionally a secular and democratic republic in which all the citizens enjoy equal rights. But things have turned out somewhat differently.

During the periods of Muslim and British colonization, other religions of non-Indian origins besides Christianity and

Islam came in as well, including Judaism, Zoroastrianism and Baha'i. In addition, a number of indigenous religious movements also came into existence, of which the best known were Lingayatism in the South and Sikhism in the North. All these religions upheld the principle of equality for all human beings. But instead of helping to bring about a genuine change in the condition of the Dalits, all of them helped to maintain the status quo already established by the Hindu Brahmanical caste system. Why did these latter religious traditions, despite their ideals, fail?

The social and religious conditions during the thousand years of Muslim domination of India, from about 700 to around 1700 C.E., show that the status of the Dalits continued more or less as it had been. Al-Beruni, a visitor to India around 1030 C.E., describes the treatment received by Dalits during this period as he observed it:

> The people called Hadi, Doma (Domba), Candala and Badhatau [names for Dalit communities given by others] are not reckoned among any caste or guild. They are occupied with dirty work, like the cleaning of the village and other services. They are considered as one sole class, and distinguished only by their occupations. In fact, they are considered like illegitimate children; for according to general opinion they descended from a Sudra father and a Brahmani mother as the children of fornication; therefore, they are degraded outcastes (*Alberuni's India*, ed. E.C. Sachau, vol. I, pp.101f.).

Recent studies have confirmed that Muslim society was itself divided into a number of different grades or classes, though these differed from the Hindu caste system. The highest social level, comparable to the Hindu "twice-born" upper castes, was made up of the *Ashrafs* ("honourable ones"), *Shaikhs* (chiefs) and Mughals and Pathans (corresponding to the Hindu *Ksatriyas*). The middle group comprised those who had "clean" occupations. The lowest echelon included the Dalit converts, who did scavenging, sweeping and other menial tasks. This would seem to explain why caste distinctions continued in Indian society during the Muslim period and why there were no changes in status even for Dalits who embraced Islam.

As far as Judaism is concerned, there are two ancient settlements – in Cochin, Kerala, in South India, and around Bombay, Maharashtra, in the west. Historically, the presence of Jews in India is confirmed from 1020 C.E. onwards, the date inscribed on a set of copper plates given to a Jewish leader named Joseph Rabban by a Hindu king, which list 72 privileges granted to the Jewish community, including the right to ride an elephant, to be carried in a litter, to be preceded by drums and trumpets and to have a crier call out before their approach so that the lowly might withdraw from the streets. The same king accorded similar privileges to a group of Syrian Christians. In effect both communities were thus given the status of caste Hindus. It seems that later on both had to internalize caste influences in order to provide legitimation for their status. During a visit to Cochin in December 1993, I learned that Jews there are divided into two main *jatis* or groups: *gora* ("white Jews") and *kala* (black or Dalit Jews). I was told that these two groups have very little social contact; in particular, they do not eat together or intermarry.

The ancestors of the Parsees, the followers of Zoroastrianism, emigrated from Persia during the 7th century C.E. Before they came to India they were already divided into four classes along the pattern of the Hindu caste system: clergy, warriors, peasants and artisans. When they arrived in India, they were allowed by the local king Sanjan Jadi Rana to settle in a place named Sanjan, in Gujarat, under certain strict conditions, which they accepted. Since the Parsees did not believe in conversion, there was little chance for them to influence the social order based on the caste system. Thus they were largely unconcerned with the problem of the Dalits.

The heartland of Lingayatism (or Veerasaivism) is northern Mysore, in the state of Karnataka. Lingayatism is an egalitarian religion in which everyone, including women, is treated as equal. Lingayats worship Shiva and, according to their rule, all members must always wear the Shiva emblem, the *lingam*. But in practice Lingayats too are divided into *jatis* or groups, which are similar to those of Hindus. Among the highest are the *Jangamas*, hereditary priests or teachers. Their impact on the Dalit problem is limited, both by the fact that Lingayatism has been limited to one small part of one Indian state and by the fact that its followers are not free from the *jati* distinction.

Also coming into existence during the Muslim period was the Sikh religion. It too upholds the principle of egalitarianism; and its founder, Guru Nanak Dev, did away altogether with caste distinctions and ceremonies. Yet a number of extant testimonies show that by the first half of the 19th century, a caste hierarchy was well established among the Sikhs. The followers of the Sikh religion today can be divided into two broad divisions, "mainline" Sikhs and the *Majabhi* Sikhs, or Sikhs by faith, who are otherwise Dalits. *Majabhi* Sikhs always have a lower social status; therefore, mainline Sikhs do not intermarry or have other normal social relations with them.

Another egalitarian religion which has come to India from outside is Baha'i. Its members are limited to some villages in central India and have been fully Indianized under the influence of Hindus. As a result, the Baha'i religion, despite its egalitarian principles, has made very little positive contribution either in bringing social change in general or in the case of the Dalits.

British rule

While the British period in India could be said to have begun with the inauguration of the East India Company in London in 1599, for the first 150 years the Company was interested only in business and trade. Only from 1744 onwards did Lord Robert Clive turn it into a military power. In 1857 a major revolt took place in the Indian army, which was dominated mainly by the upper castes who apparently sensed a threat to the caste system and its practices. Having crushed the revolt, the British, through a proclamation by

Queen Victoria, transferred political authority in India from the East India Company to the Crown in 1858. Shaken by the military revolt, the British decided to maintain the status quo and follow a policy of non-interference. Indeed, they actively upheld and supported the caste system, even providing protection to it through an Act of Parliament.

In many ways the work of Christian missionaries during the British period influenced the situation in India, particularly by challenging the various religious traditions to evaluate and rethink their approach to the poor and to Dalit groups. But in the final analysis the missionaries upheld the caste system, even accepting it within the Christian church. The support from state and church alike meant that very little could be expected to change with respect to the condition of the Dalits.

There was, however, one positive note during the British period. A number of small movements came into being which showed concern for the Dalits. Already earlier the Bhakti movement had helped the cause of the Dalits during the Muslim period, particularly in the spiritual sphere. This was largely due to the influence of the Bhakti saints, who were either non-Brahmins or themselves Dalits. Under British rule, the efforts of most of these movements tended towards reform rather than a total change. But some of the personalities who were involved directly in the struggle for change or reform did leave an impact on subsequent Dalit movements down to the present day. These included Jotiba Phule, B.D. Ambedkar and Gandhi. The first two worked for a total development of the Dalits; Gandhi's work was limited to certain reforms within Hindu society. In the next chapter we shall look more closely at the influence of both the Bhakti movement saints and these three leaders.

Ultimately the work of the reform movements, including those involving Christian missionaries, induced the British government to act. A reflection of this was the new terminology used to refer to the Dalits. The Act of 1919 recognized for the first time the existence of "Depressed Classes". In 1931, the superintendent of the census in the state of Assam suggested changing this designation to "Exterior Castes", on the ground that this was a broader title which would include not only "outcaste" people but also those who had been marginalized for some breach of the caste rules. More pertinent to our discussion – and to the struggle of the Dalits – is the term "Scheduled Castes", which was first coined by the Simon Commission, appointed by the British government, and was embodied in Section 305 of the Government of India Act of 1935.

At the outset, the term "Depressed Classes" was used more or less for all kinds of people. Not until 1932 was it applied specifically to people with an Untouchable background. Members of the minority communities – Muslims, Christians, Anglo-Indians – which the British government was trying to help, were excluded from the definition of "Depressed Classes", but special benefits were bestowed on them, including the right to their own separate communal electorates. In 1931, a special committee was set up to draw a list or "schedule" of the castes and classes to be included under the Depressed Classes, and a Round Table Conference convened in London.

The key figures at the Round Table Conference were Gandhi and Ambedkar. The latter demanded a separate electorate for the Depressed Classes (whom he always referred to as the Untouchables), proposing that they be classified as "Protestant" or "Non-Conformist" Hindus. But Gandhi objected to Ambedkar's demand for a special electorate. By this time, he had introduced his own favourite term to replace "Untouchable", namely, *Harijan* ("Children of God"). The Dalits themselves did not like this term.

As Gandhi and Ambedkar could not agree, no final decision was taken at the Round Table Conference, and the matter of a separate communal electorate was left for the Round Table Conference chair, British Prime Minister Ramsay Macdonald, to decide. In 1932 he issued the Communal Award, which replaced the expression "Depressed Classes" with "Scheduled Castes" (which henceforth became the name for the "Untouchables" and was included in the 1936

Government of India Scheduled Castes Order). Gandhi vigorously opposed the Communal Award to the Scheduled Castes, fearing that they would thus be separated from Hindu society as a whole. So he announced that he would begin a fast unto death. Since under the circumstances nobody wished to be held responsible for Gandhi's death, even Ambedkar had to give in and agree to see the Communal Award altered in a manner satisfactory to Gandhi. According to this agreement, in place of a "separate electorate", a "joint electorate" for the Scheduled Castes with the caste Hindu majority was accepted. While a chance for effective liberation and freedom was thus lost by the Dalits, Ambedkar did get some compensation in the form of a large number of seats for the Dalits.

Independence: internal colonization

The Constitution of India as a secular and democratic republic came into effect upon independence in 1947. Article 16 fully recognized the need for the development of the Dalits, both socially and educationally. It abolished the practice of "untouchability", declaring it an offence punishable by law. Every citizen of India was granted the right to profess any religion (Article 25), and among the fundamental rights of all citizens (Article 15) is the freedom from discrimination on the grounds of religion, race, caste or sex.

In addition, the Constitution granted special rights to Dalits to share political power by reserving seats for them at the central, state and local administrative levels (Articles 330-34). Economically, it not only prohibits any form of forced labour (Article 23) but also provides that a certain number of posts be specially reserved for Dalits in various departments at central and state government levels, according to the percentage of Dalits in the population. Article 46 provides for special attention to the educational and economic interests of the Dalits and for protection against social injustice and all forms of exploitation.

Besides these wide-ranging provisions, the Constitution empowers the President of India to appoint a special officer or commissioner to see the implementation of these safe-guards. Over the years, the government has passed further laws to protect the rights of the Dalits and to prevent atrocities against them, including the Protection of Civil Rights Act (1955), Protection of Civil Rights Rules (1977) and the latest Scheduled Castes (Dalits) and Scheduled Tribes (Prevention of Atrocities) Act (1989).

The protection and privileges under these laws, however, apply only to Dalits who profess Hinduism, Sikhism or Buddhism. They do not apply to Dalits who profess Christianity or Islam, because the government of India has consistently refused to grant either of these religious groups the status of Scheduled Castes. Moreover, the existence of these constitutional and legal provisions does not in itself guarantee that Hindu, Sikh or Buddhist Dalits in fact enjoy basic human rights, since the implementation of the laws is finally in the hands of their opponents, the so-called upper-caste people.

While a complete survey of the historical developments in this area over the 50 years of Indian independence is beyond the scope of this book, we shall look briefly at three key moments.

1. The Constitution (Scheduled Castes) Order, 1950

Article 341(1) of the Indian Constitution empowered the President of India "by public notification [to] specify the castes, races or tribes or parts, or groups within castes, races or tribes which shall, for the purpose of this Constitution, be deemed to be Scheduled Castes". Once the President had given such an order, the list could be changed only through an Act of Parliament.

In exercising this power, the first President of India, Shri Rajendra Prasad, promulgated the Constitution (Scheduled Castes) Order in 1950. In effect, it re-enacted the list made by the Government of India in 1936 under British rule, using the same criteria as previously. The order begins with a pre-amble, then gives a list of Scheduled Castes. The significant point, however, which has created a problem for the Dalits, is made in the third paragraph: "Notwithstanding anything contained in paragraph 2, no person who professes a religion different from Hindu shall be deemed to be a member of a 'Scheduled Caste'." This paragraph has been amended by Parliament twice: in 1956 to add the words "or Sikh", and in 1990 to add the words "or Buddhist".

The position of the President and Parliament is thus the same as that of the British government in 1932-36: "religion" is used as a criterion to define Scheduled Castes. This is a fundamental contradiction, since this criterion and the decisions made on the basis of it violate the fundamental constitutional principle of the equality of religions.

The inadequacy and injustice of using religion as a criterion to define Scheduled Castes emerges clearly in the argument made by Ram Vilas Paswan, then minister of welfare and labour, in May 1990 during discussion of the proposal to include Buddhist converts from Scheduled Caste background in the list of Scheduled Castes:

> "Neo-Buddhists" are a religious group which has come into existence in 1956 as a result of a wave of conversions of the Scheduled Castes under the leadership of Dr Baba-Saheb Ambedkar. Upon conversion to Buddhism, they become ineligible for statutory concessions... Various demands have been made... for extending all the concessions and facilities available to the Scheduled Castes to them also *on the ground that change of religion has not altered their social and economic condition*... As they objectively deserve to be treated as Scheduled Castes for the purpose of various reservations, it is proposed to amend the Presidential Orders to include them therein.

This amendment was passed by Parliament, and now Dalit Buddhists receive the same concessions which were going to Scheduled Castes belonging to the Hindu and Sikh religions. The important point to note is that the basis of this amendment has changed from what the 1950 Order said about "religion", which of course was also unconstitutional.

On the surface, the Presidential order looks progressive. But if one looks into the spirit beneath it, one can see how this order, supported by the powerful lobby of the Hindu fundamentalist religious right, has become the basis for the persistence of the problems of the Dalits. The Constitution itself may maintain the spirit of secularism by guaranteeing full freedom of religion to every citizen (Articles 25, 26, 28, 30) and forbidding any discrimination by the state on the basis of religion (Articles 15, 16, 29, 325). But the Presidential Order implementing it, which violates the sacred spirit of the Constitution, has become an instrument for dividing the Dalit community itself on the basis of religion. It should be noted that Shri Rajendra Prasad, who as India's first president promulgated the original order which violates these constitutional guarantees, was himself a member of a powerful orthodox Hindu association, the *Hindu Mahasabha*.

Moreover, the use of the term "Hindu" in the Presidential Order of 1950 has the consequence that India as a nation has officially upheld the system of caste (*varna*). In this way, what Gandhi won under British rule through his "fast unto death" in 1932 has been confirmed in post-independence India by those interested in maintaining such a system. In this way the process of what we have called "internal colonization" is strengthened.

For more than four decades, Dalits have also fallen into this trap, and those who have avoided it – especially Christian and Muslim Dalits – have been deprived even of their basic human rights and equality. To some extent, Sikh and Buddhist Dalits have also won their rights, but it seems that this has not yet paved the way for others.

2. *The first report of the Commissioner (1951)*

As mentioned earlier the Constitution empowers the government to appoint a special officer "to investigate all matters relating to the safeguards provided for the Scheduled Castes and Scheduled Tribes under the Constitution, and report to the President on the working of those safeguards at such intervals as the President may direct, and the President shall cause all such reports to be laid before each House of Parliament". In November 1950, L.M. Shrikant was appointed as the first such special officer. His first report, covering the period up to 31 December 1951, provides a helpful glimpse at the status of the Dalits in the early post-independence period. It opens by saying that

> caste in Hindu society is still the most powerful factor in determining a man's dignity, calling or profession. Such a rigid caste system is not found anywhere else outside of India. All such professions involving handling of the so-called dirty jobs like tanning and skinning of hides, manufacture of leather goods, sweeping of streets, scavenging, etc., are allotted to some castes, also known as Harijans, who are about 5 crores [50 million] according to the latest figures available.

A key statement is found on the opening page of the report:

> By the force of habit the Harijan (Dalit) has lost his self-respect to such an extent that he regards his work to which his caste is condemned not as a curse from which he should extricate himself, but as a privilege or preserve, which he must protect. He has not much courage to seek another job in a field or a factory. He has thus become lazy in mind and body and callous to his own condition; and he will not educate his children.

These words are revealing in identifying the inner nature of "Dalitness" as it has evolved under the ongoing oppression of the caste and social system which Indian society continues to maintain. This system is capable of drawing persons into a kind of self-captivity, a slavery from which it seems almost impossible to be liberated. What Shrikant describes as laziness in mind and callousness about one's own condition is part of the inner nature of Dalitness which is responsible for many of the problems of the Dalits. Such problems cannot simply be dealt with by passing legislation and providing economic opportunities. Shrikant points to one possible solution, namely education, but he goes on to suggest that Dalits are in fact typically unwilling to provide that to their children. Before talking about how to provide for the education of Dalit children, this facet of the inner nature of Dalitness needs to be addressed.

Shrikant based his report on an extensive tour around India in order to secure first-hand information about the Dalits, and much of his report is devoted to what he observed personally. For example, discussing the Social Disabilities Removal Acts which had been adopted by several states, he remarked that very few crimes committed against the Dalits had come to light. The reason for this, he suggested, is not only that the Dalits often lacked the courage to come forward but also because the police were incapable of taking action if a report was made to them.

3. The 28th report (1987)

How did conditions change over the succeeding years? Some insight into this comes from a review of the 28th report of the commissioner for Scheduled Castes and Scheduled Tribes, which in fact covered the period from 1981 to 1987, since the position of commissioner had remained unfilled for several years in the 1980s.

This report suggests that some positive changes appear to have taken place in the practice of untouchability in urban areas, but that change was very slow in coming to rural areas. According to the report, "the denial of access to a common facility like drinking water is... a normal feature. Separate settlements for members of the Scheduled Castes [Dalits] continue to be a rule in the village." But also in urban slum areas, "members of the Scheduled Castes will be found in the worst sectors".

The report also discusses the difficulties faced by Dalits who do seek to benefit from any of the constitutional or legal provisions intended to help them:

> The assertion of rights by members of the Scheduled Castes, particularly their refusal to accept humiliation, as a part of their being, is being retaliated against in many areas by other communities through the assertion of their rights inherent in the ownership of land and primacy in economic institutions, which could be challenged formally under the law. Sometimes these formal postures can be grotesque and inhuman, for example, when the right to live and even of easement are denied to those who can claim not an inch of land as their own in the village.

Reports about various kinds of disabilities, insults and other atrocities suffered by Dalit communities appear almost daily in Indian newspapers. The 1987 report catalogued such atrocities during the previous six-year period according to cases of "grievous hurt", rape, arson and other offences – totalling about 15,000 reported cases a year. It suggested that there were three main reasons for such atrocities: (1) unresolved disputes related to allotment of government land or distribution of surplus land to landless Dalits; (2) tension and bitterness created by non-payment or underpayment of minimum wages prescribed by state governments; and (3) resentment against the Dalits' manifestation of awareness of their own rights.

Concerning literacy rates among the Dalits, the 28th report showed that while this figure for the Indian population as a whole had risen from 24 percent in 1961 to 29.4 percent in 1971 and 36.2 percent in 1981, the corresponding figures for the Dalit community were 10.2 percent (1961), 14.7 percent (1971) and 21.4 percent (1981). Regarding Dalit representation in central government service, the report disclosed that there was a very thin presence of Dalits in the higher paid and higher decision-making posts. Drawing on records of the employment exchange for 1983-85, the report said that the percentage of placements remained around 8 percent of the number of registrations, and that more than half of the vacancies in positions reserved for Dalits were in fact kept unfilled.

Here we cannot go into greater detail in summarizing this report. But the information it provides makes very clear what is already evident from this brief overview: that Dalits in general, even those belonging to the Hindu, Sikh and Buddhist religions, continue to face substantial oppression and exclusion in Indian society.

* * *

To recapitulate our historical overview of the Dalit problem, the colonization of the Dalits, which began with their defeat at the hands of the Aryans, was internalized through religious myths and stories and finally by introducing a fixed social order based on a caste system dependent on one's birth. Neither the centuries during which India was successively dominated by Muslims and the British nor the arrival of other religions, including Christianity, succeeded in overcoming the influence of this caste system; indeed, the effect of Muslim and British colonization was to strengthen the status quo. With independence, the rule of the country went back into the hands of the so-called upper castes, the original colonizers of the Dalits. During the succeeding period of what we have called "internal colonization", the religious factor, used during the Aryan colonization to keep the Dalits outside the purview of the Hindu religion, has been used to dominate the Dalits by bringing them within the boundaries of Hindu religion, but only in the outermost circle, and at the same time by trying to close the way for Dalits to embrace any of the egalitarian religions, such as Christianity, Islam, Buddhism and Sikhism.

3. Struggle

Although thousands of years of oppression and exploitation have taken their toll on the Dalit communities by instilling in many an attitude of acceptance and apathy regarding their plight, it is also true that, throughout this entire history of successive "colonizations", the Dalits have sought in various ways to resist the injustice and indignities being imposed on them. In this chapter we shall draw attention to some of the highlights of that struggle down through the centuries, dividing our account into three phases.

The first phase of struggle (600 B.C.E. to 1700 C.E.) began during the Rigvedic period and continued through the Muslim era. During this early phase the foundations of Dalit struggle and of Dalit consciousness were laid. The second phase covered what might be called the British-Christian period, from 1700-1947. In general terms, the struggle of these years was chiefly concerned with the separate identity and political rights of the Dalits. During the third phase, since 1947, the Dalit struggle has centred on the solidarity of the Dalits and the vision of liberation which is now becoming more clear to them.

The Vedic and Muslim periods

The accounts recorded in the *Rigveda* make it clear that from the beginning the Dalits did struggle against their oppressors, the so-called Aryans who later considered themselves upper castes. They protested against their conditions and fought with the invaders, even though they were regularly subdued and defeated by them.

The supremacy of the Brahmins was also challenged later during the Rigvedic period by two non-Brahmin princes of the *Ksatriya* caste: Mahavira (540-468 B.C.E.), the founder of the Jain religion, and Gautama Buddha (563-483 B.C.E.), the founder of Buddhism. But their efforts did not bring much fruit as far as the Dalits were concerned, because the followers of both were unable to withstand the pressures of the caste system. The Jains were eventually obliged to formulate their own caste system on the model of the existing Hindu system. Many of the Buddhists were forced into exile in neighbouring countries, and the ones who remained came themselves to be considered untouchables by the upper-caste Hindus.

Then there was a long gap before the Dalits could see a glow of hope. Muslim dominance from the 8th century C.E. to the end of the 17th century brought no substantial change in the condition of the Dalits. Even so, this period provided an atmosphere which helped both Dalits and non-Dalits to sow the seeds of the future struggle. For example, prior to the Muslim period, the Dalits did not have the right to join the army or perform military service. This right was granted to them by Muslim rulers, some of whom even encouraged the Dalits, recognizing their bravery. Amritnak Mahar, a Dalit of Maharashtra, is well-known as a brave warrior who faithfully served the Muslim king of Bedar. In 1129 the latter granted the Mahar Dalits a charter of 52 rights, which included the right to a small collection (*baluta*) for services offered to the upper-caste Hindus. Another significant development during this period was the growing influence of Muslim mystics, *sufis*, one of whose central teachings was the equality of all human beings.

As mentioned earlier, it was during the 12th century that the *Bhakti* (devotion) movement began among the Hindus. This was a counter-movement to the existing Hindu belief that *gyan* (knowledge), *karma* (good deeds) and *dhyan* (reflection), the three ways to human salvation, were the monopoly of the caste Hindus, particularly the Brahmins. The saints of the Bhakti movement questioned the authority of the so-called upper caste and introduced the idea of devotion to God by everyone through songs, music and dance. Instead of Sanskrit, the language of the Brahmins, the Bhaktis used the local vernacular of the common people. Among the Bhakti saints were also Dalits. In South India the most prominent of these were Chokhamela and Kanaka, although they did not succeed in asserting their right to spiritual equality and were even refused entry into the temple of Vithal at Pandharpur and the temple of Krishna at Udipi. The well-known Dalit saints of the North were Namdev and Ravidas;

and the other prominent Bhakti saints in North India were non-Brahmin and lower-caste. One of them, Kabir, a Muslim by faith but a member of the weaver caste, boldly declared the spiritual equality of all human beings on the basis of their common origins:

> God in the beginning created Light,
> all human beings belong to him.
> Since from one Light is the whole world created,
> Here who is noble or who is inferior?

Guru Nanak Dev (1469-1539), the founder of the Sikh religion and a member of the Ksatriya, or warrior caste, went even further than Kabir in declaring his identification with the low caste and the Dalits:

> The lowest among the low castes,
> those still lower and the most lowest –
> Nanak is in solidarity with them;
> he does not care for the high and mighty.
> Because your grace falls on the land
> where the poor are looked after.

But the real beginning of the Dalit consciousness of their own state can be seen in the writings of the low-caste and Dalit saints themselves. According to a familiar saying in my mother tongue, Panjabi, *jis tan lage, soi jane* – "the real pain is known only by the victim". To illustrate exactly what was experienced and expressed by low-caste persons and Dalits about their state, we shall cite two examples.

The first comes from the 14th-century saint Namdev, a *Sudra* (fourth caste), one of whose writings has been included in the Sikh scriptures, the *Sri Guru Granth Sahib*. Writing about his first-hand experience of his treatment during a visit to a Hindu temple, he says:

> In a cheerful mood to thy temple I came.
> While performing devotion, I was pushed off.
> O Lord, why have you given me birth
> in the home of a washerman?
> They considered my caste very low.
> Picking up my blanket, back I turned,

and sat at the back courtyard of your temple.
I as your devotee sing the songs of your praise...

The writings of the Dalit saint Ravidas, somewhat later
than Namdev, are perhaps the first written testimony to Dalit
consciousness during the middle ages. For this reason he
later became the patron saint of a number of Hindu Dalit
groups and movements. An English version of one of his
songs, which is also found in the *Sri Guru Granth Sahib*, is
as follows:

You who are considered upper-caste!
well-known is my cobbler's caste,
but still in my heart, I continue to praise my Lord.
You should know even the wine made with sacred Ganga water
the real devotees will not drink.
Even after it gets mixed up with impure liquids,
the sacred Ganga water is not different from it.
The Tar tree is considered impure,
so also the paper made from it is considered such.
But when words of the Lord's devotion are printed over it,
it is worshipped and bowed down to.
People of my caste are hide-beaters and binders,
carrying dead animals around Banaras.
Yet upper-caste Brahmins to me make obeisance,
As Ravidas, thy servant with thy Name has taken shelter.

During the Bhakti period, which arose during the Muslim
period and continued during the time of British colonization,
the orientation of both Dalit and non-Dalit Bhaktis was to the
inherited religious traditions, in particular to a religious
reform of Hinduism. But an ideological basis for the subsequent Dalit struggle was being laid by both Bhakti saints and
Muslim sufis, in particular by the Dalit saints who declared
their equality in spirituality and their equal status before
God. The demand for total change, however, was still await-
ing.

The British period
We saw in the previous chapter that the coming of the
British to India did not really affect the situation of the Dal-
its until after the English gained military control and estab-

lished their political power following the battles of Plassey (1757) and Buxar (1764). In fact, the real change in the Dalit struggle did not take place until the time of the Mutiny in 1857. We shall thus look at this period of Dalit struggle under two phases: pre-Mutiny and post-Mutiny.

1. Pre-Mutiny

The British extended the access of Dalits to military service, giving them a far greater role than they had in the Muslim period. Two Dalit battalions were formed, including a marine battalion of the Bombay Army (1777). Similar opportunities were offered Dalits in other regions, including Bengal and Panjab. This factor would prove very important for strengthening Dalit consciousness in the future.

During this period a number of regional and sub-regional movements and programmes came into existence, in which the leadership was both Dalit and non-Dalit. Their leaders, only a few of whom we can mention here, were spread out over all of India, and included people of almost all religious backgrounds (for further information, see R.K. Kshirsagar, *Dalit Movement in India and its Leaders*, New Delhi, 1994, pp.154-375).

While it is impossible within the scope of this book to detail all the factors which helped to advance the Dalit struggle, two key factors were the open policy of the British, based on democracy and human rights, and the opportunities for education which were provided to Dalits. For the latter, the work of Mahatma Jyotiba Phule (1827-90) was particularly important. A member of the lower or backward *Mali* caste, Mahatma Phule was perhaps the first person to seek to unite "touchables" and "untouchables" in solidarity.

The conversion of Dalits to various egalitarian religions, including Christianity, Islam, Sikhism and Buddhism, was the other major development inducing followers of various religions to think about the situation of the Dalits. In different regions and states, large-scale conversion to these religions – particularly to Christianity during the British period – shook the very foundations of the Indian social order. For example, when a small group of Dalit Sikh students at the Amritsar Mission School in Panjab announced in 1873 that they were going to become Christians, this posed a real challenge to the Panjab Sikh community, as a result of which some of the Sikh leaders were forced to work for reformation within their community. In order to do that, they began in October 1873 a movement later known as the Singh Sabha Movement, one of whose objectives was to look after the needs of Dalit Sikhs. A similar impact was felt among Hindu and Muslim intellectuals and reformers.

The British also introduced new vehicles of communication, including press and publications, a new legal system, new land policies, new educational policies and industrial development. All of these factors, directly or indirectly, helped to raise the consciousness of the Dalits, particularly their leaders.

A number of local and regional Dalit movements came into existence during the second half of the 18th century and the 19th century. Here we shall mention only four. (1) *Ramdeo Panth* was begun by Shri Guru Ramdas (1726-98), who belonged to a Dalit community called *Dhed* in Rajasthan. *Ramdeo Panth* challenged orthodox Hinduism by refusing to accept the caste system or the teaching of *avataras* (incarnations). (2) Also in central India was the *Satnami* movement, begun by Guru Ghasidas (1756-1850), whose teaching included the belief in a casteless society, treating the wives of others as mothers and love for all human beings and animals. Ghasidas' belief in a formless God and his opposition to idol worship brought him into conflict with the Hindu reactionaries, who murdered him. (3) The *Nasraiah* sect was named after its founder, a Dalit Muslim who worked in Andhra Pradesh. Nasraiah's teachings stressed the importance of good moral conduct, not worshipping idols and maintaining unity among the Dalits. He died in 1825. (4) The *Matna* sect, founded by the Bengali Dalit Namsudra Harichand (1811-79), taught that one should lead an ideal family life, not follow any religious ceremony led by a Brahmin priest and not worship in any upper-caste temple.

2. The Mutiny and after

As we noted in the previous chapter, a proclamation of Queen Victoria transferred political authority in India from the East India Company to the British Crown following the Mutiny in 1857. By the time of this Mutiny, the stage was set for the growth of a national-level Dalit consciousness. The Dalit struggle became better organized in various states and regions and also spread to the masses. As their self-consciousness grew, the Dalits' insistence on civil, religious, educational, economic and political rights became more and more vocal.

In fact, according to one account, it was an incident connected with the status of the Dalits and their growing self-consciousness which touched off the Mutiny itself. A Dalit labourer asked a Brahmin soldier named Mangal Pande for a drink of water from his *lota* (canteen). The soldier refused on the ground that the Dalit labourer's touch would pollute his *lota*. "Your take much pride in your caste," the Dalit labourer retorted, "but wait a little while: the *Sahib log* [Englishmen] will make you bite cartridges dipped in cow and pork fat. What will happen to your caste then?" Hearing this, Mangal Pande is said to have run through the barracks spreading the news that the British were about to pollute both the Hindu and Muslim religions. Within no time, this rumour spread all over North India, and the result was the Mutiny.

While the uprising itself was put down, it had two immediate consequences for our concern here: the transfer of political power to the Crown and the British decision henceforth to preserve the social and political status quo by way of a policy of non-interference, whose effect was to uphold and support the caste system. Eventually they even protected the caste system through an Act of Parliament, which declared that "due regard may be had to the civil and religious usages of the natives". This position continues to be accepted by many Western Indologists even today.

Nevertheless, Dalit consciousness had taken root, and neither British policy nor an Act of Parliament could stem the growing support among the Dalits for their struggle. That the

Dalits had become conscious not only of their state of affairs but also of who they were and what had brought them to their present state is evident from the organizational steps which they took.

The first thing that became clear to them was that they were in fact the original people of India and that their present status as Dalits was a consequence of the imposition on them of the Hindu social order based on the caste system. So it became important for them to regain their original status and also to reject not just the Hindu caste system but the Hindu religion as a whole. This is the background of the various conversion movements from Hinduism to other religions among Dalits, of which the conversion of B.D. Ambedkar and his followers to Buddhism in 1956 was the climax.

Here we shall look briefly at a number of the initiatives taken by Dalits around the country during this period.

The *Adi-Dravida Mahajan Sabha*, whose members were the Dalit Pariah community, came into existence in 1890. It demanded agrarian rights for Dalits in Tamil Nadu and a lowering of the standards required for access to subordinate services. The government accepted these demands in 1894. In 1918 they demanded that their contemptuous name "Pariah" should be replaced in government records by the name *Adi-Dravida* – meaning the original inhabitants of Dravida Land. One of their main leaders was M.C. Rajah.

The *Adi-Andhra Mahajan Sabha* was begun in 1917 under the leadership of Guduru Ramachandra Rao. It addressed the Dalits in Andhra Pradesh as *Adi Andhra* (the original inhabitants of Andhra), and demanded educational rights in public schools, representation on city and village councils and boards and the provision of drinking water. A similar Dalit organization, led by K. Kelappan and C. Krishnan, was begun in Kerala in 1927, the *Adi-Keralotharana Sangham*. Its programme included the education of the Dalits and their right to walk on public roads. In 1930, the *Adi-Karnataka Sangh* came into existence; it worked along similar lines as its sister organizations in Tamil Nadu and Andhra. Among the well-known Dalit associations in North

India was the *Adi-Dharam* ("followers of the original religion"), founded by Mango Ram in Panjab in 1926. This group, which followed the teachings of Ravidas, believed that the Dalit communities known as Chamar, Churha, Sansis, Bhangrer and Bhils were the original inhabitants of India. They taught that there was no discrimination at the time of the creation of human beings, but all were equal.

Another well-known Dalit organization, which was founded in Uttar Pradesh, was the *Adi-Hindu* movement, begun by Swami Achhutanadji (Hiralal) in 1921. *Adi-Hindu*, which rejected the teachings of Brahmanical Hinduism, believed in one God and the equality of all human beings and taught that the religion of saints is the true religion of India. The so-called untouchables – the Dalits – were the original inhabitants of *Bharat* (India).

Many other organizations came into existence in other Indian states, among them the All-Bengal Namasudra Association (founded in 1912) and *Chamar Daiva Sabha* (The Church of God of Chamars-Pulayas), a Kerala-based Dalit organization which opposed the treatment given to Dalit Christians by the so-called upper-caste Syrian church. It was active until 1950.

But there is no doubt that the most important figure of this second phase was Bhimrao Ranjio Ambedkar, known among his followers as Baba Saheb Ambedkar. Born on 14 April 1891 in Mhow in central India, he joined the Dalit struggle in 1919 and dedicated the rest of his life, up to his death on 6 December 1956 in New Delhi, to working for the Dalit community. Already in the previous chapter we have noted the important role he played in the Round Table Conference in London in 1931. Although he lost out to Gandhi after the latter undertook his "fast unto death", he did succeed in getting a larger representation for Dalits in various state and central assemblies.

Ambedkar believed in the total liberation of the Dalits. To achieve this goal he prescribed a formula which included self-organization, education and protest. One of his main methods of work was the formation of political parties: the first attempt was the Independent Labour Party, formed in 1936, and the second the All-India Scheduled Castes Federation (SCF) in 1942. His main goal in these efforts was to get a share of political power, which he believed was necessary in order to bring about a change in the existing social order. He made the purpose of SCF very clear:

> I am definitely of the opinion that in this country, political rights must be shared between the Hindus, the Muslims and the Depressed Classes. The Depressed Classes must by law have a proper share in the government of the country along with the Hindus and Muslims. The future Constitution can only work if it rests on these three pillars. To achieve this you must all come together under one flag and have only one organization. If we so far have not achieved the position in the Constitution which is due to us, it is because we have not united. If you all unite and work under one organization, I have no doubt that you will reach the position you are entitled to.

The SCF thus sought "attainment by the Scheduled Castes of a status as a distinct and separate element in the national life of India and to obtain for them their political, economic and social rights to which they are entitled by reason of their needs, their numbers and their importance".

Membership of SCR was restricted to the members of the Scheduled Castes, and it put up candidates only for those seats which were reserved for the Scheduled Castes. It had functioning branches in the Panjab, Uttar Pradesh, Bengal, Madras and the central provinces and continued to exist until 1956, when Ambedkar decided to disband it, having decided to form another political organization which would not be limited to Scheduled Castes. But this takes us into the third, post-independence, phase of the Dalit struggle.

Post-independence

The real momentum of the Dalit struggle developed in the post-independence period and, as we have already seen, the main champion at the outset was Ambedkar. In the first cabinet of independent India, headed by Jawaharlal Nehru, Ambedkar was appointed minister of law. He was also elected chairman of the drafting committee of the Constituent Assembly on 29 August 1947; indeed, he was largely responsible for drafting the Constitution, which was adopted on 26 November 1949 and implemented on 26 January 1950.

We saw earlier that this Constitution offered the Dalits, after nearly 100 years of organized struggle, a wide range of social, educational, civil, religious, economic and political rights. But as we also saw, since the implementation of these rights was left in the hands of the so-called upper castes, these gains were mostly on paper. For this reason, the story of the struggle of the Dalits has continued in the post-independence period in the form of political parties, protests and the struggle for unity and solidarity.

1. Political parties

After founding the SCF in 1942, Ambedkar went on to organize the People's Education Society in 1945 in order to promote higher education. As a result, a number of schools and colleges were started in Maharashtra. He challenged his followers and other Dalits to "educate, agitate and organize" in order to achieve their fuller liberation. Ambedkar led a number of protests, climaxing in October 1956 when he and a large number of his followers publicly embraced Buddhism, as a final act of total rejection of the social and religious order of Hinduism.

Ambedkar's last effort to bring together Dalits and other oppressed groups in Indian society was through a new political party. He had originally intended to give it the name "People's Democratic Party", but he was persuaded to call it instead the Republican Party of India, on the ground that the word "People" was increasingly being identified internationally with Marxism. The Dalits were not in sympathy with the Communists, who had never been friends of the Dalits, largely because of the class character of the Communist leadership.

Unfortunately, after preparing the constitution for the party and circulating it to leaders of the Scheduled Castes, Ambedkar died in December 1956. The RPI was formally founded in 1957 with a number of prominent leaders. It became a growing force in Uttar Pradesh, Madhya Pradesh, Panjab and especially Maharashtra. Its strength and its widening base alarmed the leaders of the Congress Party, who thus set about trying to weaken it, fearful that it might join with one of the other opposition parties like *Jan Sangh*. Congress Chief Minister Y.B. Chavan befriended RPI leader B.K. Gaekwad, who was easily taken in. Two of the demands of the RPI were that the reservations for Scheduled Castes be extended to Buddhists and that the *Deeksha Bhoomi*, the place in Nagpur where Ambedkar had embraced Buddhism, be allotted to the Buddhist organization to construct a memorial. This seemed a small price to be paid for their support, and the Congress government led by Chavan acceded to these terms.

The formation of a Congress-RPI alliance for the forthcoming elections had far-reaching effects. A split occurred in the RPI. Some of its leaders justified the alliance on the grounds that Congress was basically liberal and secular. Others proposed going even further to join Congress. These leaders attached a great deal of importance to presence in the legislature and seats in the cabinet, which otherwise would have been out of reach because of the nature of the electoral system and the expenses involved. Two prominent RPI leaders – D.T. Rupwate and R.D. Bhandare – joined the Congress Party. The most prominent leader in the North, B.P. Maurya, was elected on the RPI ticket in the first election, but after the end of his first term also joined Congress. Rupwate was made a minister, Bhandare was elected to Parliament and later appointed governor of Bihar. Maurya was also appointed as minister, but he had lost the support of his Muslim and Dalit followers and could not be elected thereafter. All this factionalism weakened the RPI, which already had few resources and a limited following, thus doing enormous harm to the great work started by Ambedkar.

Frustrated by these developments some young Dalits began to focus on written expressions of protest. Like many black writers in the US at the time, they began by depicting the horrible conditions in which the Dalits lived and worked and the atrocities committed against them in the villages. A militant movement patterned after the Black Panthers in the US was begun in Maharashtra. Dalit poems, stories and novels began to elicit recognition in the Hindu press. Visiting villages where atrocities against Dalits had been committed by upper-caste people, the Dalit Panthers also launched a campaign to agitate for an election boycott.

These activities led to the recognition of the Dalit Panthers as a new force in Indian politics. Although the manifesto they released (from which we quoted in chapter 1) reflected Marxist influence, most of the Dalit Panthers felt an allegiance to Ambedkar and opposed the Communists. However, despite their sharp criticism of many RPI leaders for their intemperance, acting contrary to the legacy of Ambedkar and consorting with Congress members, the Panthers themselves suffered from factionalism. Many of those facing criminal charges for violent acts then did not hesitate to approach individual members of the Congress Party to have their cases dismissed.

The All-India Samata Sainik Dal, which had been founded by Ambedkar, was revived by Bhagwan Das and his colleagues in the Ambedkaria movement. Bhagwan Das had also founded the Ambedkar Mission Society to promote the ideology of Ambedkar. In Delhi he established the United Republic Party and contested elections under its banner. This succeeded in unifying some small factions, but it failed to bring the major factions closer together.

New leaders emerged. Prakash Rao Ambedkar formed the Republican Party (Prakash) and tried to attract a following. He is still working to create a strong base among the Dalits, other "backward classes" and religious minorities. But he lacks strong party machinery and a clear-cut ideology or programme which might attract people.

The Bahujan Samaj Party (BSP) was founded by Kanshi Ram in the late 1980s. Ram introduced himself to the Dalits by forming the "Backwards and Minority Communities Employees Federation". Though on the whole he does not have a clear-cut ideological basis, the BSP did succeed in electing two members of Parliament in 1990 and, through an alliance with backward class people, in polling 10 percent of the votes in Uttar Pradesh, returning 12 members to the state legislature. The party improved this showing in 1993, retaining 67 seats in the assembly and forming the state government with the Samajwadi Party of Mulayam Singh. Later it broke away from the Samajwadi Party and, with the help of the upper-caste Bharitya Janata Party (BJP), formed its own government, which included the first Dalit woman to be a chief minister. But the BSP failed to unite the Dalits, and when the BJP withdrew its support after less than four months, the Uttar Pradesh government fell.

2. *Protests and protest literature*

Some historians have seen the mass conversion of Dalits during the last quarter of the 19th century and the first quarter of the 20th century as the beginning of the modern Dalit movement. It is true that protest which takes the form of rejection of the past and of a religious system is particularly forceful. The paramount case was Ambedkar's embrace of Buddhism in 1956. Another took place on 19 February 1981, when 220 Hindu Dalit families in the village of Meenakashipuram in Tamil Nadu embraced Islam, basically to protest the ongoing exploitation of Dalits by caste Hindus and the atrocities committed by the police. The Meenakashipuram Conversion, as it came to be known, received attention from almost all Indian political parties – Congress, Janta Dal, BJP and RPI, as well as various regional parties in South India – with only the RPI supporting it.

There are many more examples of protests and civil disorder. Anti-Dalit riots broke out in 1978 after a decision to rename Marathawada University for Ambedkar. When the state government passed a resolution to this effect, the upper-caste opposition took this as a symbol of the emergence of Dalit power. Hundreds of Dalits had their houses burned and many Mahar Dalits lost their lives. Regarding the 1978 riots, Dalit poet Mina Gajbhiye wrote:

I had sutured with difficulty the weeping wound of centuries.
Those stitches are all ripped out, ripped out by Marathawada;
even our old bonds of give-and-take are snapped.
From now on, I won't scream, "I want to live!",
From now on I'll live to die.
Let the village become a burning ground with me.
I will not live like a dog, nowhere.

Dalit protest literature has been an effective way for Dalit writers to express their Dalit consciousness and show their inner feelings. Over the years, writings about the Dalits by others, especially of course their opponents, have generally portrayed them as objects. This was already the case in the Vedic literature. But the Dalit writers' consciousness has made real progress in redressing the balance and portraying the Dalits as the subject of their own history. Their works include poetry, autobiography, short stories, essays and speeches.

A leading role in this flowering of Dalit literature has been taken by Marathi Dalit writers. Two anthologies with translations of their work into English appeared in 1992: *Poisoned Bread*, edited by Arjun Dangle, and *An Anthology of Dalit Literature*, edited by Mulk Raj Anand and Eleanor Zelliot. These works, besides revealing in a very human way the deeply rooted inner agony of the Dalits, also show that the Dalits have broken the centuries-old silence imposed on them by the caste-structured society. A few excerpts may give an impression of the changing status of the Dalits in human history.

We used to be their friends
when, clay pots hung from our necks,
brooms tied to our rumps,
we made our rounds through the upper lane
calling "Ma-bap, Johar, Ma-bap"...

Today we see a root-to-crown change,
Crows-jackals-dog-vulture-kites
are our close friends.
The upper lane doors are closed to us.

"Shout Victory to the Revolution!"
"Shout Victory!"
"Burn, burn those who strike at tradition!"

An editorial note accompanying this poem – "Revolution", by Arjun Dangle – points out that the line "'Shout Victory to the Revolution' is a quotation from a Brahmin poet. Dangle's point is that while the elite call for revolution, those who revolt are burned."

The truth that Dalits have recognized themselves as full human beings, as the subjects of their own history, emerges from these lines in Sharan Kumar Limbale's poem "White Paper":

I do not ask
for the sun and moon from your sky,
your farm, your land,
your high houses or your mansions.
I do not ask for gods or rituals,
castes or sects,
or even for your mother, sister, daughters.
I ask for
my rights as a man...
My rights: contagious caste riots
festering city by city, village by village,
man by man.

For that's what my rights are –
Sealed off, outcaste, road-blocked, exiled.
I want my rights, give me my rights.
Will you deny this incendiary state of things?
Uproot the Scriptures like railway tracks,
Burn like a city bus your lawless laws...

My friends,
My rights are rising like the sun.
Will you deny this sunrise?

In addition to these more literary works, systematic attempts are now being made to reach directly to the historical roots of the Dalits. Ambedkar himself made a beginning in this direction in his many speeches and writings during the

1930s and 1940s and then in his major work in 1948, *The Untouchables*, which dealt specifically with two questions: "Who were they? Why did they become untouchable?" He hinted at the common roots of three groups of Indian people, which he called the Criminal Tribes, the Aboriginal Tribes (Tribals) and the Untouchables (Dalits):

> What can be said of a civilization which has produced a *mass* of people who are taught to accept crime as an approved means of earning their livelihood, *another mass* of people who are left to live in full bloom of their primitive barbarism in the midst of civilization and a *third mass* of people who are treated as an entity beyond human intercourse and whose mere touch is enough to cause pollution?

Ambedkar insisted that Dalits, whom he called "broken men", are equal to Hindus racially.

Two more recent works which present Dalits as a subject are *The Untouchable Story*, by D.P. Das (1985), which gives a good picture of the agonies which Dalits in India must suffer, and my own monograph *Roots: A Concise History of the Dalits* (1991), in which I have sought "to identify the time or period from which the Dalits of today started losing their identity. Because at that particular time the history of Dalits began. Prior to that they were not in a Dalit state; they were normal human beings enjoying their full self-identity."

To regain their full human self-identity, Dalits must become the subject of their own history. The responsibility of regaining that identity rests with the Dalits themselves; and for this their struggle and protest must continue.

3. The Dalit Solidarity Programme (DSP)

Behind the formation of the Dalit Solidarity Programme lie the efforts carried on during the past two decades by numerous organizations, action groups and individuals. But in a deeper sense, the DSP has grown out of the pressure of the awakening brought about by the Spirit among Dalits themselves towards their solidarity – which was already there although they were not aware of it. It is true that a good deal of enabling support came from the World Council of

Churches, but it is also true that the pressures of the Spirit and of the Dalits themselves have helped the WCC to reach the point where it was able to open itself to receiving the agenda and the guidelines from the Dalits.

The position of the WCC on this issue became clear during the Council's seventh assembly (Canberra 1991). In its statement on "Indigenous Peoples and Land Rights – Move Beyond Words", the WCC said: "We affirm the growing consciousness of indigenous peoples' struggle for freedom, including those of the Dalits of India." The "we" in this declaration included representatives of Indian churches – the Church of North India, Church of South India, the Mar Thoma Church and others.

To fulfil this mandate, the WCC's Programme to Combat Racism approached representatives of various Dalit groups, who told the PCR that the Dalits themselves would prepare the agenda and inform the WCC about the areas in which assistance was needed. To prepare this agenda, about 120 delegates representing the different sections of the Dalits and belonging to different faiths (Christian, Buddhist, Hindu, Muslim and Sikh) gathered in a national convention in Nagpur, central India, at the end of December 1992. For the first time in the history of the Dalits, they detached themselves from religious barriers to come together to prepare themselves to fight a common fight against their common suffering and oppression, because they shared the common heritage which they have named "Dalit".

Together the delegates to the Nagpur convention prepared a four-point agenda: (1) to strengthen solidarity among Dalits all over the country; (2) to extend full cooperation to the efforts of the indigenous people of India to secure their full rights; (3) to liberate the educational system, which has been used as an instrument of oppression; (4) to internationalize and create awareness in the international community about the discrimination, oppression and loss of human dignity of the Dalits. The DSP working methodology would include publications, seminars and workshops, lobbying and exchange of visits both nationally and internationally.

The convention appointed a national working committee of 35 members, with Bhagwan Das, a Buddhist scholar and Supreme Court advocate, as president and myself, a Church of North India presbyter, as secretary-director. To widen regional representation 17 other members were added; and two new officers appointed: Dr Swarna Latha Devi as national officer for women and Prof. A. Ramaiah, a young Dalit Hindu, for national youth activities. The committee meets annually in October to decide programmes and budget. Regional and sub-regional conveners work in different areas and states. Besides general programmes for implementing the four-point agenda, the DSP also carries out special programmes for women and youth.

During 1993-94, regional consultations and mass public meetings were held in Shimla (Himachal Pradesh) for the northwest, Bombay (Maharashtra) for the west, Trivandrum (Kerala) for the south, and Sarnath (Uttar Pradesh) for central and east India. In addition, a national conference of Dalit women was held in Delhi, and a national workshop for Dalit youth in Yelagiri Hills (Tamil Nadu). These activities were expanded in 1994-95 at state and district levels in all regions. In addition to a range of smaller events and meetings, three major activities were organized: a workshop in Gujarat to introduce alternative teaching methodologies to 60 Dalit educators; a May 1995 consultation on common Dalit ideology at Batala (Panjab); and the first national consultation of Dalit and indigenous people in Ranchi (Bihar).

At its October 1995 meeting DSP decided to continue efforts at the local, village and town levels through 1997, with its second national convention planned for December 1997.

In working towards its overall objective of regaining the collective identity of Dalits, which ultimately will lead to their whole liberation, the role of the Christian church and Christian theology is extremely important. To this we turn in the succeeding chapters.

4. Theology

While "Dalit theology" may be one of the youngest expressions of theology in the world, its roots go back to the beginning of Dalit history. This is evident from our discussion in the three preceding chapters. We saw in the opening chapter that "Dalits" are part of God's overall plan for the redemption or liberation of human beings; indeed, the prophetic message refers to the "Dalit" community by name as part of God's concern (cf. Isa. 11:4; Zeph. 3:12). Our discussion of Dalit history in chapter 2 exposed how the Dalits' opponents, particularly their first colonizers, rooted their effort to separate the Dalits from other human beings in a theology which severed relationships between the Dalits and God. In surveying Dalit "struggle" in chapter 3, we saw that the early Dalit saints like Ravidas sought to re-establish the relationship of their community with God. All the movements of conversion, to Christianity and to other religions, grew out of this quest.

Therefore, if theology is critical reflection on the relationship of God and human beings in different historical circumstances, one can trace the roots of Dalit theology back to the very dawn of their history. At the same time, Dalit theology is something new, for it was only during the 1980s that a few Dalit Christian thinkers began to make serious attempts to express themselves theologically, based on their personal and communal experiences as Dalits who were directly involved in the actual struggle of their people. Among these early writers on Dalit theology were Arvind P. Nirmal, M.E. Prabhakar, Bishop M. Azariah, K. Wilson, V. Devasahayam and the present writer.

In answering the question of why a Dalit theology is necessary, we must begin by recognizing that the dominant Christian theologies in India, both European-based "systematic theology" and contemporary Indian Christian theology, do not address the issues Dalits face in their daily life or fulfil the Dalits' needs. These European and Indian theologies are in effect expressions which respond to the experiences and needs of the rich and the elites of this world, those who are hierarchically near the "top". For the Dalits, who have been forced to the "bottom" by the same elites whom these other theologies serve, they are irrelevant. Thus when Dalit theologians speak of Dalit theology, they are in fact making an affirmation about the need for a theological expression which will help them in their search for daily bread and their struggle to overcome a situation of oppression, poverty, suffering, injustice, illiteracy and denial of human dignity and identity. It is these realities of Dalit life which require the formulation of a Dalit theology.

When the term "Dalit" is used to modify "theology", it is a pointer to the role of this theological expression. "Dalit" refers to the situation in which the people who use this term for themselves are living. This is an oppressive state in which they have been forced by their opponents to live for centuries. Those who realize this personal and communal state of oppression call themselves "Dalit". The main factor behind this realization is their history, which is what has helped them to know about their lost identity of the past, which their opponents have tried to destroy. From this history they have also learned how their oneness has systematically been destroyed by introducing among them hundreds of human divisions and giving them names according to the numerous low-level tasks assigned to them. This has forced them to engage themselves in a quest for solidarity in order to regain this oneness. But finally it is Dalit theology which will help them to place the various actions of the past and the present into a theological context as an assurance that what they have done or are doing are right in the sight of God.

Traditional Indian theologies

Until now there have been two dominant expressions of Christian theology in India. The one arrived with the European missionaries and in time it came to be, under the name of "systematic theology", the major area of theological study in the country. The other is the traditional "Indian Christian theology", which basically came into being as a result of efforts made by some of the so-called upper-caste converts as a response to their faith. Both these expressions have largely followed the Greek connotation of the expression "theology" – the study of God, or *Brahman*, or Pure Being.

In his classic work on Christian theology, John Macquarrie listed the six formative factors of classical (European) theology as experience, revelation, Scripture, tradition, culture and reason. As the source of their theology, the traditional Indian Christian theologians have followed classical Hinduism: *pramanas* (authorities), *Sruti* (inspired scriptures), *anubhava* (personal experiences of God) and *anumana* (inference or reason). Neither of these systems has much directly to do with human history. In the case of the first there are two histories – sacred and profane (human); in the case of the second, history basically has no meaning, because classical Hinduism gives history no place. Hinduism talks of history as a cycle which moves on from one great age or *yuga* to another, until at last the wheel turns full circle and returns to the beginning; it has no purpose or progress.

It should be noted that some of the later Indian Christian theologians, including P.D. Devanandan and M.M. Thomas, have taken into account the usefulness of history. For example, Devanandan says in one of his works:

> In fact Hindu religious thought has consistently maintained that Absolute Being is totally transcendental and, therefore, in every way unrelated to world life and history. This would mean that the Hindu indifference to history is due to its characteristic theology, its conception of history of which they may not be conscious themselves, but the role played by them in the Indian life is part of this shift.

What M.M. Thomas says about the relationship between history and Christian theology is clearer:

> Living theology is the manner in which a church confesses its faith and establishes its historical existence in dialogue with its own environment. If the Indian church is understood merely as a product of Western missions, these Indian theologies will only appear as an appendage to Western theology. Now that we are beginning to discover that the Indian church has a history of its own, we are also beginning to discover an Indian Christian theology with its own history.

In his book *The Acknowledged Christ of the Hindu Renaissance* (Madras, 1970), M.M. Thomas developed this theme of "living theology", arguing that it must be born out of a "dialogical situation". It must work

> not in isolation from, but in dialogue with the new Hindu philosophy and theology; that is, by restating the fundamentals of the Christian faith positively within these terms, which at the same time restructures the truths in neo-Hinduism on Christian foundations. This is the cultural significance of all attempts at indigenous Indian Christian theology.

Nevertheless, while both Devanandan and M.M. Thomas highlighted the role of human history in the construction of traditional Indian Christian theology, they continued, like their predecessors, to operate within the ongoing traditions of Hinduism.

Liberation theologies

The four theologies which we shall take as examples in this section share a common name, "liberation theologies", because they not only identify a common historical base from which to operate but also have a common goal, namely the total liberation of the whole people. Dalit theology shares these criteria. These four theologies – Latin American liberation theology, black theology in the US, Korean-born *minjung* theology and the "theology of struggle" in the Philippines – have taken shape from the pains, struggle and oppression of the common people. In that sense they are sisters – perhaps we should say "older sisters" – of Dalit theology.

Among Latin American liberation theologians perhaps no one has been clearer about the role of human history in constructing a theological expression than Gustavo Gutiérrez, whose *A Theology of Liberation* (1971, English translation 1973) is certainly one of the seminal theological works of our time. Right at the beginning, Gutiérrez, reflecting on the ancient biblical text, says:

> In the first place, charity has been fruitfully rediscovered as the centre of Christian life. This has led to a more biblical view of

the faith as an act of trust, a going out of one's self, a commitment to God and neighbour... Love is the nourishment and the
fullness of faith, the gift of one's self to the other, and invari-
ably to others. This is the foundation of the praxis of Christians,
of its active presence in history. According to the Bible, faith is
the total response of man to God, who saves through love.

Gutiérrez is not in fact saying anything radically new
here. Rather, he is calling our attention to the twofold "great
commandment" of the Christian faith: "Love the Lord your
God with all your heart, soul, mind and strength, and your
neighbour as yourself" (Mark 12:28-31). Both the application and implementation of this commandment take place in
human history, giving wholeness to faith as a response to
God. This process of Christian faith functioning through
human history Gutiérrez calls "historical praxis". Making the
point more explicitly, he says that "the Christian community
professes a 'faith which works through charity'. It is – at
least ought to be – real charity, action and commitment to the
service of men. Theology is reflection of a critical attitude."
History, as mentioned earlier, has been divided into two: one
part dealing with the issues of other-worldly history, one
dealing with the issues of this world. But Gutiérrez insists:

There are not two histories, one profane and one sacred...,
rather, only one human destiny, irreversibly assumed by Christ,
the Lord of history. His redemptive work embraces all the
dimensions of human existence and brings them to their fullness. The history of salvation is the very heart of human history.

Gutiérrez' point about the oneness of history is very
important for Dalit theology if it intends to attack the "dalitness" of the Dalits, which has been reinforced in their psyche
by the traditional theological expressions.

In an essay on "Black Theology and Black Liberation",
James Cone, like Gutiérrez, upholds the role of "history" in
the construction of theology. Indeed, he makes the point even
more forcefully:

Black history has arisen to establish an authentic black past.
Unlike European immigrants who came to America seeking
escape from unjust tyranny, Africans' presence was not by

choice; we came as bondsmen, chained in ships. It was the slave-experience that shaped our memory of this land... Unfortunately, our slavery was not limited to physical bondage. Added to physical domination was the mental enslavement of black people – the internalization of the values of slave-masters. We were required to deny our African past and affirm those European values responsible for our enslavement. At the worst, this meant accepting the slave-condition as ordained by God.

How is black history related to black theology? Cone's answer is as follows:

Black history is recovering a past deliberately destroyed by slave-masters, an attempt to revive old survival symbols and create new ones. Black power attempts to shape our present economic, social and political existence according to those actions that destroy the oppressor's hold on black flesh. Black theology places our *past* and *present* actions towards black liberation in a theological context, seeking to destroy alien gods and create value structures according to the God of black freedom.

This is similar to our situation as Dalits – except that whereas the history of African-American oppression goes back about 500 years, the history of the Dalit people's oppression has continued for more than 3500 years, during which we have lost virtually everything.

In his book *Messiah and Minjung* (1992), Korean theologian Kim Young-Bock describes the *minjung*, the ordinary masses of people, as the true subjects of history:

The discovery of the *minjung* led not only to the realization that it is the *minjung* who are the perceiving subjects of real historical experiences, but also to the understanding that the *minjung* are the subjects in the making of history. They bear the historical burden to sustain human societies. They work, they cultivate and they serve... The sustenance of human life, the creative process in cultural life, the transforming dynamics of the social and political processes are fundamentally based upon the endurance and suffering sacrifice of the *minjung*. Therefore, their suffering becomes the foundation of the society, and they sustain the ups and downs of the historical processes.

The reality of the *minjung* as "subjects" of history is important for us as Dalits, because this realization is the first step towards the recovery of lost human dignity by any historically oppressed community.

The people of the Philippines have also gone through a very painful and oppressive historical experience. In constructing a Filipino expression of what he calls a theology of struggle, Eleazar S. Fernandez also begins with a rereading of history from the perspective of his oppressed people:

> My reading claims to be a reading from below – from the experiences of those whose history has long been muted. It is a reading derived from the experiences of those who are daily threatened by another kind of trinity: the absence of breakfast, lunch and dinner... The history of the Filipino people is a history of struggle against the negative forces, both within and without, that continue to abort the people's cherished dreams... This struggle is the struggle of the whole people, some of whom may not profess a Christian belief... Christians must learn to work with those with whom they do not agree on everything, but agree on something that is vital... Out of the involvement of Christians in the struggle of the whole Filipino people, the theology of struggle has struggled to be born. From this womb of struggle it came to see the first light of day, and from its cradle it has been nurtured. Born in and out of the struggle, it has no life apart from this struggle; it has taken shape in and out of the struggle; and it cannot be properly understood apart from this struggle. Its basic presuppositions, shape and content all bear the indelible mark of this involvement in the wider struggle.

In this statement, too, lies a challenge for Dalit Christians. Unlike the Christians in the Philippines, we are a very small minority, so it becomes more pertinent for us as Indian Dalit Christians to be involved in the wider struggle of the Dalits, to be partners in making our common history, which will ultimately be the womb from which Dalit theology is born.

Dalit history and Dalit theology

Our discussion so far in this chapter has offered a number of important pointers for the formation of a Dalit theology. In

looking at the two traditional forms of Indian Christian theology we saw that we must set these aside, if not reject them
completely. The Greek philosophical ideas in which Western
systematic theology is deeply rooted have distanced it from
a biblical understanding and prophetic interpretation of history. Indian Christian theology, on the other hand, has been
rooted in Hindu Brahmanical philosophical systems which
do not care for the reality of human history. This makes it
irrelevant for the Dalits, and its non-historical approach
makes it alien to the biblical historical truth. Both of these
theological expressions are centred on ideas, not actions.

Our brief look at four examples of liberation theology
(and we might have chosen others) has helped us to understand the role of history in the construction of Dalit theology.
But this in turn poses questions regarding the history of the
Dalits and the sources, particularly written materials, available for Dalit history. That leads then to questions about the
unity or solidarity of Dalit communities and where Dalit
Christians find themselves within this solidarity. Besides
these and other questions, perhaps the most important one for
Dalit Christian historians and theologians is how to deal with
the biblical story from the Dalit perspective. All these are
basic and important questions, which one has to tackle while
working on the construction of Dalit theology. In this section
we shall look briefly at the questions related to history, then
take up the questions related to Dalit solidarity in the next
section.

The importance of history
When asked about Dalit history, some Indian leaders are
inclined to say that "we should not talk about the past". In
other words, we should basically *forget* our history. Among
those outside the church who espouse this view are political
ideologues who are afraid of losing the power they have,
which stems from the influence of the upper castes or
classes. Similarly, some of the church leaders who think this
way are persons who hold power within the church structures
by virtue of being converts from the so-called upper castes.

Other Indian Christian leaders have been taught by Western theological education to dismiss this history. But besides these two groups there are church leaders who are themselves of Dalit origins who believe that we should "forget our history" out of a fear that they or their forebears will be exposed. Of course, they too have been brainwashed by the old missionary thinking that everything that we had – our religious beliefs, ideologies and practices – was evil and contrary to Christian faith. Such people also suggest that reminding ourselves of our past means going back to where we started.

Over against the appeal to forget our past, no matter how this call may be explained or defended, is the reality that it is only our past, our history, which can teach us about our identity. This is particularly true for those in Indian society who are not only living a life of deprivation and poverty but also have lost their very sense of being human. I refer of course to the Dalit communities. Many Dalits look as though they have recovered their lost humanity and dignity, either because they have been educated, or because they have achieved a certain level of economic success. Still, the vast majority of these people remain mentally poor. Their attitude towards their own self is not fully human. Mere economic betterment and formal education are not enough to regain full humanness. However, it is precisely such measures to which the efforts of the Indian government, most non-governmental organizations and the Christian churches have largely been limited.

This is why history is so important for us as Dalits. Neither general historians nor religious historians nor church historians have represented the views of our people. But we need to know our past, which alone will reveal to us that we were also full human beings once, enjoying all the benefits of a normal human being – land and property, natural resources, dignity and freedom. This will not be possible until our history is written from *our* point of view, the "view from below". What has been written so far about Dalits – whether history, theology or ideology – has been written from "above", by Christians from an upper-caste background or by Europeans.

There is a biblical parallel which underscores the importance of knowing history to an enslaved people, a people to whom God gave liberation and of whom God made a "great nation". The God who liberated Israel also commanded them to teach their past history of slavery and liberation to their children from generation to generation:

> When your children ask you, in time to come, "What is the meaning of the decrees and the statutes and the ordinances that the Lord God has commanded you?", then you shall say to your children, "We were Pharaoh's slaves in Egypt, but the Lord brought us out of Egypt with a mighty hand... If we diligently observe this entire commandment before the Lord our God, as he has commanded us, we will be in the right" (Deuteronomy 6:20-25).

The Bible also tells us that whenever this nation ignored that commandment, God sent them back again to a life of slavery, and when they realized their mistake God liberated them anew. In this sense, the Dalit Christians of India have not begun our history, because in general we have continuously denied our past. St Paul also reminds Dalit Christians that we should always remember our past, how God, out of nothing, has made us a "something", a people (1 Cor. 1:26-28).

Sources of Dalit history

Having underscored the importance of recovering our history, we must immediately go on to acknowledge that reconstructing and writing Dalit history is an extremely difficult task, because our Dalit forebears have left nothing in written form. Whatever written records are available were produced by our opponents. This is particularly true of the literature produced during the Vedic period (1500 B.C.E. to 700 C.E.), especially the *Rigveda* and the *Manusmriti*. These works offer abundant evidence that among the basic rights taken away from the Dalits during this period was the right to education, rendering them unable to write their own stories. This ban continued even after the Vedic period.

In the absence of written sources of their own, Dalits have no choice but to depend on the materials produced by their opponents. Here the science of hermeneutics is indispensable, for it enables a rereading, from a Dalit point of view, of materials written by the Dalits' opponents and of the later historical data recorded by Western Christian historians, including the many reports prepared for the different mission boards whose personnel were at work in India. The same techniques can be applied to the various translations of and commentaries on the Bible in Indian languages, which generally have not represented the perspectives of Dalits.

It is beyond the scope of this book to enter into the actual exercise of such a rereading, but in two of my own earlier works I have sought to apply this kind of hermeneutic to biblical and historical materials in order to construct a history of the Dalits: *Roots: A Concise History of the Dalits* (Delhi, 1991), and *Towards Dalit Hermeneutics: Rereading the Text, the History and the Literature* (Delhi, 1994). The latter focuses on selected Old Testament passages which use the Hebrew root *dal* (some of this has been incorporated into the first chapter of this book); and also seeks to interpret mission histories in order to understand why the Christian gospel has remained at a distance from the actual life of Dalits.

These hermeneutical exercises have helped to show that the oppressive situation in which Dalits live today is neither something of their own choice nor an ordinance of God. Rather, these conditions have been imposed on them by their opponents, first by physical defeat, which made them *dasa* (slaves), then by taking away their basic human rights one by one, including education, thus mentally enslaving them. But ultimately it was not the oppression which destroyed the Dalits; it was in fact their own acceptance of their oppression at the hands of their opponents, so that they consider their inferior status to be part of the natural order of things.

Yet the opponents of the Dalits have not succeeded in fully destroying the humanity of the Dalits. The question is how much of a collective effort Dalits can now make to construct their own authentic Dalit history from their own point of view, through their own eyes as victims. What is called for is thus a journey into the unexplored depths of Dalit consciousness. The theological expression that grows within the womb of this Dalit history will then lead to actions that will ultimately result in Dalit liberation.

Finally, we may note that some of the source material for Dalit history is scattered in the form of stories about past and present Dalit Christians. Among the great pioneers of the Indian church were such Dalit Christian heroes as Vethamanikam of Travancore (Kerala), Venkayya of Kistna (Andhra) and Ditt of Sialkot (Panjab), to whom we shall refer in greater detail in the next chapter. Though generally ignored or forgotten, for Dalit Christians they are primary historical sources. Over and above this are the personal stories and testimonies of Dalit Christians today, in which God can very clearly be seen working in human history. These histories also serve as a source of future hope for the resurrection of the Dalit community.

Dalit solidarity

While the term "solidarity" is very similar in meaning to the "historical praxis" of which Latin American liberation theologians such as Gustavo Gutiérrez speak, I believe it is a more suitable expression for rediscovering, in the Indian context, the core message of Christian faith from the Dalit perspective.

Pope John Paul II's 1987 encyclical on social concern, *Sollicitudo Rei Socialis*, defines solidarity as "a commitment to the good of one's neighbour with the readiness, in the gospel sense, to 'lose oneself for the sake of the other'". The pope goes on to describe solidarity as "undoubtedly a Christian virtue" which has many points of contact with charity, "which is the distinguishing mark of Christ's disciples". This has evident parallels with the quotation from Gutiérrez cited earlier concerning the rediscovery of charity "as the centre of the Christian life".

But what does it mean to say that "solidarity" is our action in response to God? To begin with, it means that God has first shown God's own "solidarity" with human beings in history. This solidarity with us was not just an idea, but took the form of concrete actions in human history, to which the Bible witnesses. This action in history began with God's first act of creation (Gen. 1); and in Genesis 2, we see God in full solidarity with human beings while visiting them in the Garden of Eden. But then the concrete reality of sin enters human history (Gen. 3). The expansion of human sin as an historical reality is reflected in Genesis 4-11.

Thereafter we read of God's intervening directly in human history by calling Abraham (Gen. 12). To concretize God's action of solidarity, the Bible writers chose the case history of a nation, Israel, which over time became a slave people in Egypt. Seeing Israel's suffering and oppression at the hands of the pharaohs, God decides to help them through Moses. In commissioning Moses, God says explicitly, "I have observed the misery of my people who are in Egypt. I have heard their cry on account of their taskmasters. Indeed, I know their sufferings, and I have come down to deliver them from the Egyptians" (Ex. 3:7,8). Thus God's solidarity with the oppressed takes the form not only of words or ideas, but of action: in "coming down to deliver them", God became part of their struggle. This action shows God taking sides: that of the oppressed against the oppressor. This was not so much a religious action as a political act with economic and social dimensions; and we read in Exodus how God, through Moses, fought against the Egyptians until the Israelites received their liberation. Later, the Old Testament goes on to show how God continued to be involved fully in the history of Israel and other nations through prophets and kings, but also through ordinary men and women.

The climax of God's acting in solidarity with human beings, particularly the oppressed of this world, can be seen in the act of incarnation, summarized in the familiar words of John 1:14: "And the Word became flesh and lived among us." God identified with human beings, not just by becoming a human being, but by becoming part of human history and making his home among us. The account of the incarnation in the gospel of Luke gives a more concrete picture of this solidarity of God with us; here we see the human child "wrapped... in bands of cloth and laid... in a manger" (2:7). The gospel of Matthew links this with an Old Testament prophecy from hundreds of years earlier regarding God's participation in human history: "the young woman is with child and shall bear a son, and shall name him Immanuel" – "God with us" (Isa. 7:14).

So here, in the act of incarnation, we do meet God, in full solidarity with us, not just as any human being, but as one who gave up his other-worldly identity completely for our sake and became the poorest of the poor – in a real sense, a Dalit. The model of solidarity we find in God's incarnational act in history challenges us as Dalit Christians to follow it, so that the experiences we share with the Dalits in general should become the basis of an authentic Dalit theology.

Christian Dalits can also take a clue from the experience of the Philippines, where the theology of struggle has been born from the womb of a common struggle of people of different faiths and ideologies who, Fernandez says, "do not agree on everything, but agree on something that is vital" – the common experiences of suffering and struggle of all Filipinos. The same is true for the Dalits in India. Being in solidarity with our fellow Dalits of different faiths and ideologies is a demand which the God of the Bible, through his own act of incarnation, places on Dalit Christians. This is an important factor for the authenticity of the Dalit theology, enabling it to become an instrument of destroying the social and religious structures responsible for the Dalits' ongoing historical captivity.

Dalit theology

The first thing to remember about Dalit theology is that, like other liberation theologies, it is a theological expression born from the historical experience of an oppressed people and from their encounter with the God of the Bible, who has always been biased towards the oppressed and the poor. It is rooted in the assumption that the Dalits are the makers of their own history, the subject of their history rather than the object of the histories told by others who have oppressed them.

In a real sense, it is the Dalits of Indian society who represent the undivided humanity of the divinely created world. Dalit theology is intended to enable them to recover this original state of theirs, which their opponents have tried intentionally to destroy. We have seen the concrete effects of this onslaught from their opponents on the humanity of the Dalits, and how it has led to the loss of all their other rights. The recovery of these rights now depends on their solidarity, because it is only through a commitment to solidarity that they can generate power among themselves to face the challenge of their opponents. This two-sided solidarity – with God and with fellow-Dalits of any religion, creed or ideology – is in a real sense the subject of Dalit theology.

Three elements play an important role in the reflection of Dalit theology on this relationship of solidarity among Dalits: (1) the aspiration of Dalits for their fuller liberation, (2) the recognition that God is on their side and is interested in empowering them to work for the transformation of this world, and (3) the conviction that Jesus Christ, in whom God concretely became human, is the model for this struggle and continues to struggle alongside people today through his Holy Spirit.

Dalit theology should not be seen as a "counter-theology" to European-constructed systematic theologies or traditional Indian Christian theology, for these theologies were not intentionally formulated as enabling theological expressions to deal with the Dalit experience, nor were they based on Dalit life in the past or present. Nor, as some Indian theologians have suggested, is Dalit theology interchangeable with any of the other liberation theologies. We have seen that there are obvious links on the issue of history and on the general goal of the entire liberation of the whole people. But on the issues of actual history, context, racial elements, ideological basis, all liberation theologies differ from each other and differ from Dalit theology.

For example, our African brothers and sisters in North America were brought there by force, not by choice. Black theology has grown out of oppression based on a master-slave relationship with racial roots. By contrast, most of the Latin Americans who forged today's liberation theology out of the crucible of economic oppression were of the same racial background as their oppressors; their theology is based on an economically based class system. *Minjung* theology is the outgrowth of the pain of ordinary people in Korean culture: their frustrations, agony, suffering and resentment, along with their hopes, aspirations and struggle. The theology of struggle in the Philippines is based on suffering whose roots are in political colonization. With Dalit theology the situation is different. Unlike these other communities, the Dalit community has lost everything – land, culture, language, religion, political and social rights. The Dalit story of oppression is also much longer than that of the others. For the Dalits, everything must begin anew. Their oppressors have become not only the owners and masters of the resources that belonged to the Dalits but the owners of the Dalits themselves. Thus the enslavement of the Dalits, to which Dalit theology must respond, is multi-faceted.

These differences in the historical context show that Dalit theology cannot simply be grouped together with any other kind of theology. At the same time, Dalit theology also has a different role from the others. In concluding this chapter, we may identify five elements of this role:

1. Dalit theology must address the Dalits themselves about their state and their dawning consciousness of themselves. It can help in raising the awareness that they are the remnant of a casteless community which was based on the divinely established principle of equality, in contrast to the divisive caste system created by human beings. It must also heighten their understanding that the status of inferiority assigned to them is neither of their own making nor ordained by God. Thus Dalit theology must prepare the Dalits of all religions for rejecting the old Brahmanical religious order which has perpetuated their captivity.

2. Dalit theology must also address non-Dalits, both within the church and outside of it, because those who oppress or oppose or ignore the Dalits have to that extent lost their own divinely created humanity. The role of Dalit theology in this sense is to make others aware of the suffering and pain of the Dalits and their role in it.

3. Dalit theology has a role to play in raising the consciousness of the Christian community as a whole. Current traditional theologies have undergirded the churches' support for existing political, social, economic, religious and cultural orders, including caste-based divisions, and have helped to maintain the status quo also in the church. Dalit theology must challenge the church to change.

4. Dalit theology must enable ordinary Christians to take an active role in the struggle of the Dalits. At present most ordinary members of most Indian churches seem convinced that it is against the teaching of the Christian faith to join any movement or struggle. But as we have seen, our Lord himself, in his incarnational act of solidarity, pointed to the dimensions of our calling in situations of suffering and injustice.

5. Finally, Dalit theology must create the possibility of fuller liberation or salvation, based on the Christ-event of redemption. What is called for is not merely freeing people from oppressive structures, not merely making them the subjects of their own history, not merely assuring them of the forgiveness of sins, but achieving full salvation.

5. Church

Several times in the preceding chapters we have alluded to the church's role in the Dalit issue, especially perhaps in the previous chapter, where we saw that Dalit theology arises in a context in which traditional expressions of Christian theology have had the effect of maintaining or deepening the oppression of the Dalits. Just as a new theology is needed, it seems that a new identity for the church must also be found if the church is to be part of the struggle of the Dalits.

At the outset, we should note that, in terms of its composition, the identity of the Indian church can be defined as "Dalit", because the large majority of its membership comes from Dalit background. One rough estimate has suggested that about 12 million of India's 20 million Christians are Dalits. In some states, the percentage is much higher: in my own home state of Panjab, for example, it is more than 95 percent. But this issue of the identity of the church requires a somewhat closer look if we are to understand what might be the role of the church in the Dalit issue.

The Dalit roots of the Indian church

From the many available case histories providing first-hand information about the roots of the Indian church, we shall look here at only two – one from North India, one from South India – then offer some commentary on these.

1. Ditt, the founder of the church in Sialkot (Panjab)

The story of Ditt began when the missionary J.S. Barr baptized a man named Nattu, a Hindu of the *Jat* caste (a Panjabi upper caste), on 17 November 1872. Nattu was the son of a *lambardar* (village head) and the legal heir to his father's property and position; consequently, the missionaries were very happy about his conversion. This soon turned to disappointment, however, when Nattu forfeited the right to be his father's heir. For the missionaries he proved a failure, "a weak brother". Little did they know that Nattu would become the instrument for bringing into the Christian fold a person who would later be one of the main leaders of the Panjabi Christian community. This man's name was Ditt.

Ditt was born around 1843 in the small village of Sha-habdike, about 50 km. from Sialkot (now in Pakistan). Andrew Gordon described him as "a man of the low and much-despised *chura* tribe..., a dark man, lame of one leg, quiet and modest in his manners, with sincerity and earnest-ness, well expressed in his face". By profession Ditt was a dealer in hides. He came in contact with Nattu, who taught him about Jesus Christ; and in June 1873 Nattu took him to Sialkot for baptism.

The missionary in Sialkot, Samuel Martin, was hesitant. After all, Ditt's Christian faith was based on the teachings of the "weak brother" Nattu. At the same time, Ditt's knowledge of Christianity was quite sound, and he appeared to Martin to be an honest person. In any case, when Martin suggested that they delay the baptism, Ditt was unwilling. In the words of Gordon: "Mr Martin finally decided to baptize Ditt, not because he saw his way decidedly clear to do so, but rather because he could see no scriptural ground for refusing."

At once, Martin faced another problem: immediately after the baptism Ditt asked permission to go back to his vil-lage. This was something new for Martin. The practice was that new converts would remain for a time in the mission compound for more instruction and protection. Martin was worried about how this poor illiterate man would deal with the opposition he would inevitably face in his village. In the end, however, Ditt returned to Shahabdike, and this decision proved the starting point for a Christian movement among the ex-*churas* (Dalits) of Panjab.

On reaching home, Ditt did face bitter opposition. His fel-low villagers accused him of having become a *Sahib* (gen-tleman) or a *be-i-man* (one without religion). His own sister-in-law said: "Alas, my brother, you have changed your reli-gion without even asking our counsel; our relationship with you is over. Henceforth you shall neither eat, drink, nor in any way associate with us. One of your legs is broken already, so may it be with the other."

Unfazed by the opposition, Ditt witnessed to his new faith in Christ openly and boldly, both to his family members and others. The result was amazing. Three months after his baptism he took his wife, his daughter and two neighbours to Sialkot for baptism, walking 50 km. to introduce his family and friends to the missionaries. Fully satisfied by his examination, Martin baptized them.

Ditt's work as a dealer in hides took him to many different villages. Wherever he went on business, he preached about Christ also. In the eleven years after his baptism, he brought more than 500 people from his caste into the Christian faith. By 1900 half the people of his community had accepted Christ, and by 1915 almost all the Dalits known as *churas* of Sialkot district had become Christians.

2. Vethamanikam and the church in Travancore (Kerala)

Vethamanikam was born in one of the Dalit communities of Travancore, which was at that time (the late 18th century) an independent state. His father died soon after his birth, and he was brought up in the village of Mailady by a very pious mother, who taught him to read and write and gave him a basic education. She also introduced him to high moral values and helped him to love his family God. Even in the later years of his life, he built a temple for his family God. He read religious books, including the *Puranas*.

In search of truth, he went on a pilgrimage with his nephew to the temple of Chidambaram. But while there he discovered that the life of the priests was not holy. During the night, he had a dream which convinced him that Chidambaram would not be able to help him in his search for truth. On the way home, he and his nephew stopped at Tanjore, where his married sister lived with her family. Both his sister and her husband were Christians; and it was here that Vethamanikam first heard about Christ.

On Sunday while standing outside the church he heard the singing and the message. At the end of the service, the missionary came to talk to him. Vethamanikam told him all about his pilgrimage and said that it seemed as if the Almighty God had sent him to Tanjore. While reading a small booklet which the missionary gave him, Vethamanikam was filled, he said later, with "deep joy and satisfaction... My Lord and Saviour Jesus Christ... touched my heart and it melted before God. A light from heaven shone upon my darkness and I did not want to leave the place."

After staying at Tanjore for some time more, reading more literature and asking more about Jesus, Vethamanikam was finally convinced that he had reached his destination in search of truth and had found the true Saviour. He was baptized. After remaining for a little longer to receive further guidance, Rebecca J. Parker writes, "he felt he was ready to return and take the good news to his own place; and, staff in hand, he turned his face homewards".

Back in Travancore, Vethamanikam was asked by relatives and friends, "Where are the holy gift of the Lord of Chidambaram and the sacred ashes?" Holding in his hand a copy of the gospels, he answered, "Lo, here is the Holy Gift of the Lord of all worlds!" Parker adds:

> From that time forward Vethamanikam gathered round him day by day such as were willing to hear more of the good news he had brought, and to them he read and expounded the Scriptures. This patient teaching at last won its way to their hearts... and eventually they decided to join Vethamanikam... A couple of hundred believers were thus gathered together... He gave Christian names to the members of his family... Many listened and were won to join the growing band of believers.

However, strong opposition to Vethamanikam arose within the Hindu community. He was excommunicated from his caste and persecuted in many ways. His life and property were at risk. News of his suffering and persecution even reached the royal family, but Vethamanikam decided to take his case to the highest authority. While he was reading the Bible, he prayed with these moving words:

> O Lord, dear Lord! When I worshipped idols which have no life, thou didst reveal thyself to me, a great sinner. Thou didst pass by the rich, the learned, the honourable people, and didst choose me to be thine. Now teach me, O Lord, what should I do? Put me in thy right path, and let me know what I should do

in this difficulty. Is it thy will that the light which has begun to shine here should be quenched?

Vethamanikam received an answer to his prayer. Refusing to sell his property, he decided instead to make another pilgrimage to seek help from his friends in Tanjore. There he learned to his surprise that God was already preparing a missionary to help him, who was then in Madras learning the local language. After completing his study, the missionary, William Tobias Ringeltaube, came to Mailady on 25 April 1806, with the permission of the maharajah of Travancore. In Parker's words, "the heart of Vethamanikam was at rest. He had done his best. He knew that he had been led by the Spirit of God, and he gladly handed over to Ringeltaube the work that he had so well begun."

Finding a group of believers whom Vethamanikam had prepared for baptism, Ringeltaube baptized them and appointed Vethamanikam as their catechist. For the next ten years the two worked together, and in 1816, when Ringeltaube left Travancore for reasons of health, he put Vethamanikam in charge of the whole mission. He held the church in Travancore together until December 1817 when another missionary, Charles Mead, arrived in Mailady.

During the early years only the Dalits from Sambavar responded to the call of the Spirit, but by 1819 a Spirit movement had also begun among the Nadar community of Travancore.

3. Comments on these two histories

Although the work of early missionaries and Indian Christians contributed much in general to the life of the Dalits in India, it had very little positive influence on the situation of the Dalit Christians. One could even say that the effect of the work of such early missionaries as Roberto de Nobili, Ziegenbalg, Bishop Middleton and Alexander Duff on the future church of Dalit Christians in India was negative. The same can be said about the role of some upper-caste Indian Christians, which worked against the interests of the

Dalits. For example, the three men – H.C. Mookerjee, Amrit Kaur and Jerome D'Souza – who represented the Indian Christian community in the drafting of the Constitution following independence in 1947 failed to support equal rights for Dalit Christians.

Christian missionaries went to India for the same reason as they went anywhere else in the world: to proclaim the gospel of Christ and to win human beings to faith and obedience in him. But things did not turn out exactly as they had expected. At first most missionaries were interested in preaching only to upper-caste people. Andrew Gordon, a pioneer missionary to Panjab from the United Presbyterian Church in the US, admitted in 1888, after his first 30 years of missionary work: "I began with my eye upon the large towns and cities, but have been led from them to the country villages. I began with the educated classes and people of good social position, but ended among the poor and the lowly."

By 1885, after more than 50 years of proclaiming the gospel, there were only 477 communicant members of the church in Panjab – and many of them were not Panjabis. Thereafter, we see a rapid change, with numbers continuing to grow. It is important to understand this change, which is illustrated by the story of Ditt. In the beginning it not only troubled the missionaries, but also shook Panjabi society as a whole. While this development clearly reveals the working of God's Spirit and God's option for the poor, the lowly and the downtrodden, this "Spirit Movement" was at first not taken as a happy sign by Christian missionaries in Panjab, who were distressed that so few people from the upper castes were accepting the gospel.

It seems that the missionaries were not interested in the Dalits becoming Christians. Just how troubled some of them were about the way God's Spirit was working is disclosed in a March 1884 letter to his mission board by J.C. Ewing, who described this trend of poor, low castes becoming Christians as "raking in rubbish into the church". Other missionaries even hesitated to mention these converts' social background in their reports. Still others described them as "common villagers" or "illiterate menials".

This attitude of the missionaries to the conversion of the Dalits left a negative impression which still affects many Panjabi Christians, who are afraid that talking about the past will reveal the low social status of their origins. Thus even though the missionaries later accepted the trend as a reality of their mission work, many remained unconvinced. For the sake of a few from the so-called privileged castes, they were forced to maintain double standards in the church.

The problem surfaced most visibly in worship services and around the communion table, which were, after all, the only occasions when the two groups of Christians could meet. According to Mark Juergensmeyer, they sought to resolve the problem in Panjab in two ways –

> by establishing worship services for those who spoke English and those who spoke only Panjabi, which *de facto* eliminated the lower castes from English-speaking services; or failing this by ensuring that upper-caste converts would sit at the front of the church, so that they would use the communion implements first, before they become polluted by the Christians of lower castes (*Religion as Social Vision*, Berkeley, 1982, p.186).

During my stay in the city of Jullundar in the early 1970s, I was told that the system of reserving front benches for the privileged ones had been abolished only a few years earlier.

Besides these administrative methods to deal with the problem in church services, the missionaries also used another method: that of establishing "mission compounds" in the towns, Christian colonies in cities and "Christian villages" for rural people. These settlements were intended to isolate new Christians from other people, who were considered to be heathens. Establishing separate places for these Panjabi Christians helped to create a very distinctive Christian culture and also projected an image which reflected the culture of the low people.

But despite the missionaries' hesitations, the conversion process continued under the influence of the Spirit and today in Panjab there are about 250,000 Christians on the Indian side, of which 99 percent come from the Dalit background. The majority of Panjabi Christians are on the Pakistan side, and they share the same background.

The story of Vethamanikam makes even more clearly the point about the work of the Holy Spirit in the life of Dalit individuals and communities. As a serious seeker of truth, he went from place to place before arriving in Tanjore, where he had a direct encounter with the gospel of Christ. Then he devoted years of dedicated work in Mailady before the first missionary arrived there in 1806. The kind of struggle Vethamanikam went through and the way God upheld him through his Spirit was a sure proof of the Spirit's work, not only in his life, but in the life of his Dalit community.

These are, as I have said, only two cases. One could also look at the story of Venkayya (1811-91) of the Kistna district of Andhra Pradesh. Venkayya became Christian in 1849. Mr Darling, the missionary who baptized him, had not made a single convert during his first seven years of work, because, according to J. Waskom Picket, "his eyes were upon the high-caste Hindus, and he preached to them and had personally sought out individuals among them with constant diligence, but lack of interest discouraged him". But after Venkayya's conversion, God's Spirit began working. By 1901 there were more than 29,000 Christians in Kistna District, by 1911 nearly 50,000 and by 1928 the Anglican Church alone counted 122,500 members.

In short, as Picket says, "the real founder of the church in Travancore was not Ringeltaube, but Vethamanikam. In Kistna it was not Darling, but Venkayya. In Sialkot it was not Gordon, but Ditt." This testimony is indeed a living proof of the Dalit roots of the Indian church.

The church of the Dalits

The present identity of the Indian church is portrayed well in several recent surveys and statements. For example, the 1978 report of the Inculturation Commission of the Jesuit Conference of India is very explicit about the image and identity of this Roman Catholic order:

The Society's massive investment of men and resources in the educational apostolate in India makes it inevitable that the Jesuit image is mainly derived from our men in education and from our educational institutions. A large urban thrust doubtless characterizes Jesuit educational service in the country; its favoured medium of instruction is English, and the sector of the human community served by it is comparatively the more privileged one. Whether we like it or not, all these factors combine to project an elitist image – values of the "upper ten" – to the point of successfully obscuring truly evangelical values, while uprooting and alienating us from the values of the majority of our people.

A similar acknowledgment comes from a 1993 synodical report, "Towards a Holistic Understanding of Mission", by the Church of North India:

Despite the majority of the membership of the church consisting of the marginalized, it has been primarily serving the interest of the elite and upper ten percent through the educational, medical and other institutions... The church also generally reflects the culture and values of the dominant systems.

Significantly, what these two major Indian Christian church traditions have just realized was stated fifty or sixty years earlier by Ambedkar, though it seems to have gone unheeded, if not unnoticed, by the church. In his essay on "The Condition of the Convert", Ambedkar wrote:

Indian Christians are drawn chiefly from the Untouchables and, to a much less extent, from low-ranking Shudra castes. The social services of missionaries must therefore be judged in the light of the needs of these classes. What are those needs? The services rendered by the missionaries in the fields of education and medical relief are beyond the ken of the Indian Christians. They mostly benefit the high-caste Hindus... If this is so, then the money and energy spent by the Christian missionaries on education and medical relief was misapplied and does not help the Indian Christians. The Indian Christians need two things. The first thing they want is safeguarding of their civil liberties. The second thing they want is ways and means for their economic uplift.

These statements confirm that the Indian church is, both theologically and in its physical and sociological reality, "the church of the Dalits", but that somehow it continues to project an "elitist" image or identity. Living in this contradiction, the church in India has failed either to make any real impact or to fulfil the need of the Dalits or Christians in general in India.

The intellectual underpinning of this elitist identity is the traditional theological understanding we discussed in the last chapter. It seems that structurally as well the church has reflected the heritage of the "Christendom" model of the church, which came into being at the time of the emperor Constantine the Great (280-337) and was based on the image of the Roman empire. Adopting this model, the church accommodated itself to the power of the state, which offered it patronage, in return for which the church offered legitimacy to the power of the state. Church authorities began to imitate the day-to-day life of the Roman empire and to consider themselves "princes of the church", dressing in imperial robes and sitting on thrones, in keeping with the social standing which their position in the church gave them. The choice of this model in India has prevented the Christian church from being the church of the poor or the church of the Dalits; and unless there is a structural change in the life of the Indian church, it will be very difficult for it to return to its original Dalit roots and to play the role assigned to it by its founder and Lord, Jesus Christ.

A church of the Dalits will still respect state authorities, but it will refuse to accommodate itself to the state. We must emphasize here that a church of the Dalits will not mean a church exclusively for Dalits. It actually means a church for all people of God, but with a definite preference for the Dalits and other similar marginalized groups of human society. It means a church in solidarity with those who historically have been victims of a social and religious system of oppression, according to the example of Jesus Christ. A church of the Dalits will follow the life of a prophet-servant.

Back to the roots

If the church in India wishes to play a meaningful role in the life of the Dalits, it will first have to go back to its original roots and replace its centuries-old Christendom model with a freshly discovered historical and contextual model based on Dalit realities. A radical change, a genuine paradigm shift in mission outlook, is needed in order to become an authentic, prophetic church, truly committed to Jesus crucified and to the mission he entrusted to it in India.

Keeping these insights in mind, we may conclude this chapter with a few suggestions about the role of the church in the Dalit issue.

1. The first suggestion has to do with the choice of a model for the identity of the church in India. It is evident that the problem of the Dalits, especially the Dalit Christians, is fundamentally a theological issue, rather than merely a social problem. So far, the church has ignored the biblical model for dealing with the Dalit issue. A number of stories in the Bible – ranging from Gideon (Judg. 6-8) to Hannah (1 Sam. 1-2) to Mary (Luke 1) – might furnish elements for such a model; but the complete model which covers all the aspects of the Dalit issue is the incarnational model, summarized in John 1:1-14 and Luke 2:1-7, to which we referred in the previous chapter. This incarnational model obliges the church to shun the Christendom model, which has obscured the real identity of God as human being. In the biblical incarnational model we see God dealing with the Dalit situation by himself becoming an ordinary human being, one who, according to Isaiah, "had no form or comeliness" (53:4). This act of God brought God into complete solidarity with the Dalits. God became the poorest of the poor as a human being – God became a Dalit – in order to make all the Dalits of this world rich (2 Cor. 8:9). This model challenges the church in India to rediscover the lost human identity which God took on himself. But rediscovering and accepting this model means taking part in the struggle of Dalits. It also means taking the risk of losing an identity it has become comfortable with and shunning the understanding of the Christian faith it has inher-

ited. This means accepting and recognizing the problem of the Dalits, both within the church as well as in society, both spiritually and socially.

2. The second suggestion is that Christians in India look more closely at their doctrine of the church. Is the church confined to the major "organized" churches? Or does the body of Christ represent much more than that, the whole people of God? Can the Indian church become the church of the Dalits and the poor? Is the church willing to take up the cause of those who in fact make up more than 60 percent of it, who form the body of Christ and are Dalits? Such a redefinition of the church is a necessary basis for any role to be played by the church in the Dalit issue. The church must become partners with Dalits directly. This means taking sides and taking risks. The church must abandon its policy of caution, which instead of helping the poor Dalits goes against them.

3. The third suggestion is that the church redefine its concept of mission, which at present is largely limited to saving souls. Its mission must be holistic in nature. This will also help the Dalits in safeguarding their civil liberties and their will to provide for their own social and economic uplift. Also the church must look again at its own institutions and programmes, acknowledging that at present most of them continue to support the values of the "upper-ten", who mostly represent the oppressors. The church cannot fulfil its commitment by keeping silent or by trying to restrict its responsibility to "religious" matters, as though these had nothing to do with political, economic and social issues. That understanding of mission of course well suits the powerful, both inside and outside the church, who profit from the status quo.

4. Finally, the church in India should know that millions of Dalits in general, and about 1.5 million Dalit Christians, are still waiting to receive the whole of salvation, because so far they have only been offered the half of salvation which speaks of "saving their souls". To reach these people with the "full gospel" which changes the whole person is the responsibility of every Christian representing the church in India or elsewhere in the world. The Christians and the churches,

both nationally and internationally, can indeed play an effective role in the Dalit issue provided they are willing to be in solidarity with the Dalits by following the incarnational model of Jesus Christ himself.

6. Liberation

The common theme of liberation has run throughout this short book. In this chapter we shall conclude by enumerating briefly the four stages through which the Dalits must pass before achieving the full liberation which is the goal of their struggle.

Establishing a common identity

The Dalits of India are perhaps the world's foremost example of a community which has been forcibly deprived of its identity. As we have seen, their opponents have done this work very systematically, using all kinds of means of oppression to see to it that the Dalits have lost all their human rights – religious, cultural, economic, political, linguistic, educational – and thus their identity. The first step towards their liberation is thus for them to regain the identity they have lost. That is why recovering their forgotten history is so important, for this is their only way of finding out who they were and who they are. The brief sketch in chapter 2 was a partial approach to this question.

On the basis of their rediscovered history, Dalits can claim today that there was a time when they had all their rights and were "normal human beings". The ultimate goal of the Dalit struggle today is to achieve their humanity, which in a real sense is for them the meaning of liberation. But in order to reach that liberation, they must have a common identity, because as it stands they have nothing in common to bind them together. Today they are different in all aspects – religion, colour, life-style, language and ideology. Contemporary Dalits live under hundreds of identities, which makes it almost impossible for them to do anything together, even to carry on a common struggle.

But it is encouraging to see that because of the struggle through which they have already gone, Dalits have come to a stage at which they can identify a unifying factor which has helped them to name their common identity. This factor is their common, ongoing, cumulative historical suffering and oppression, which has socially degraded them, politically disenfranchised them and economically enslaved them. To this history of oppression they have applied the common name "Dalit".

Becoming conscious of their state

The very fact that the majority of the Dalits have accepted a common name in order to express a common identity is the proof of their becoming aware of the condition into which their opponents and oppressors have systematically pushed them. Excluded from the caste-structured society, the Dalits were, for their opponents and oppressors, "outcastes". In fact, they should rejoice in having been left outside the purview of a society structured according to caste, since this means that they remain as representatives of the original casteless human community, which God created in the beginning, based on the principle of equality. This realization on the part of the Dalits is the most important factor for regaining their original human state. They are the only human beings left from the original Indian society.

It cannot be denied that some Dalit communities have to a certain extent also become divided, whether because they have followed the model of the dominant society or because their opponents have applied the policy of "divide and rule" on them. But since there is no religious sanction behind the division among Dalits, dealing with this problem is not as difficult as in the case of other sectors of Indian society.

Unfortunately, their physical defeat at the hands of the first colonizers consigned the members of the casteless Dalit community to becoming serfs and menials in society, through a systematic process sanctioned by the Brahmanical Hindu religion. Subsequently, their conquerors used other methods to defeat them mentally. But it is the acceptance of oppression, not oppression itself, which destroys people. This is exactly what has happened to the Dalit community: they have accepted the inferior status assigned by their colonizers.

Therefore any programme of education for liberation for the Dalits must have four functions: (1) to make them aware of the Dalit state into which they were forced; (2) to raise their consciousness of being part of a casteless community based on a divinely established principle of equality; (3) to heighten their awareness that their assigned inferior status was imposed on them by a humanly created system, not by their own fault or by divine creation; (4) to help them to reject the mythical Brahmanical order which has perpetuated their captivity.

Being in solidarity

Dalit solidarity is the next important step towards liberation. We said in chapter 4 that the recovery of the rights and dignity of which the Dalits have been deprived depends on their commitment to solidarity, which will generate among them the power to face the challenges of their opponents. This solidarity, we noted, has two dimensions: a commitment to God and a commitment to their fellow-Dalits of all religions, creeds and ideologies. To attain this solidarity the Dalits must organize themselves and work hard.

The process towards building this solidarity has already begun. We noted in chapter 3 that Dalits from different religious backgrounds – activists, intellectuals, doctors and other professionals, grassroots workers, women, men and youth – have been working together at the national level since December 1992. Bringing them together was not easy. Members of different religious groups, veterans of the struggle and latecomers to it, Dalits and non-Dalits – all had doubts about one another. But thanks to the spirit behind the movement, the misconceptions are being cleared up, doubts are reducing, trust is being built and cooperative work is taking place. Through consultations at various levels, Dalits have come into contact with hundreds of fellow-Dalit activists and intellectuals, who have become a regular part of a nationwide network ready to carry on the struggle in various forms.

The Dalits are also aware that their oppressors, as in the past, continue to use various means – conquest, divide-and-rule, manipulation, destruction of Dalit culture – to keep them in their ongoing captivity. These four means of oppression are being countered by introducing networking for cooperation, creating unity among the different Dalit communities and constructing a common ideology which can help Dalits to organize themselves for the common struggle and empower them to achieve the final goal of liberation.

Entering into the process of liberation

About fifty years ago Ambedkar identified the three major reasons why Dalit Christians were unable to raise a movement for their liberation. First of all, he said, there was a complete absence of desire on the part of educated Christians – both non-Dalits and the few Dalit Christians who had received an education – to take up the cause of the Dalit community and fight for it. Second, the "mental makeup" of the Dalit Christians inhibited them from breaking the bonds of the identity forced on them by the past. Third, Dalit Christians had not grasped those teachings of the Christian church which might have created in them the urge for change. Of course, these three basic prerequisites for raising a movement to change – the presence of leaders, the will to change and the theological or ideological basis on which to change – are equally applicable to the Dalit movement in India as a whole. It is encouraging to observe the extent to which Dalits in general have come to understand the need for these elements.

As the previous five chapters have made clear, their vision of future liberation is thus also becoming clearer to them. We may conclude, therefore, by summing up the three most important elements of a Dalit vision of liberation:

1. Both Dalits and their oppressors have been equally dehumanized – the former because of the oppression meted out to them by the latter, and the latter because they have adopted a value system which is oppressive in its very nature and prevents them from being able to work out liberation, either for themselves or for the Dalits. Such engagement is not just unnecessary for them, but would in fact go against their own interests. Liberation for the Dalits would destroy the very system on which they have depended to maintain

their status, which gives them the power to oppress and exploit the Dalits. Liberation is what the Dalits need; therefore, it is they alone, and the power created by their weakness and struggle, which will liberate them and their oppressors.

2. Some members of the so-called high-caste community have discovered the oppressive side of their own community. Many of them find this discovery extremely painful. This does not automatically mean that they have a genuine solidarity with the Dalits. Even if they join the struggle of the Dalits, some find themselves unable, because of their "upper-caste" instincts, to identify fully with the Dalits. This is often because they are unable to put their complete trust in the Dalits' abilities; as a result, they always believe that they must be the ones to execute the transformation. Through playing this kind of role, the struggle of the Dalits is only partially engaged. Nevertheless, members of the so-called upper caste can play a constructive role in the struggle of the Dalits as well as their own, provided that they first put their full trust in the abilities of the Dalits and avoid treating them paternalistically, then show a willingness fully to enter into the Dalit situation and finally demonstrate their readiness to commit, as it were, "caste-suicide" – which means wholly rejecting the system to which they belong and entering fully into the struggle to work *with*, not *for* the Dalits.

3. Most important, it has become clear that many members of the Dalit community, particularly those who have moved upward in life, have been carrying within themselves the model of the oppressor, which is fundamentally individualistic in nature. Many Dalits in fact aspire to be like their oppressors; some would even like to replace them if given the chance. If that is the goal of the struggle, they will lose their humanness a second time. The Dalits must rather free themselves and free their oppressors and participate in creating a new human being, one who is neither oppressor nor oppressed but, on the contrary, a person in the process of liberation.

The Risk Book Series from WCC Publications deals with issues of crucial importance to Christians around the world today. Each volume contains well-informed and provocative perspectives on current concerns in the ecumenical movement, written in an easy-to-read style for a general church audience.

Although any Risk book may be ordered separately, those who subscribe to the series are assured of receiving all four volumes published during the year by airmail immediately upon publication – at a substantial savings on the price for individual copies. In addition to the four new titles each year, occasional "Risk Specials" are published. Although subscribers are not automatically sent these books as part of their subscription, they are notified of their appearance and invited to purchase them under the same advantageous conditions.

If you wish to subscribe to the Risk series, please send your name and address to WCC Publications, P.O. Box 2100, 1211 Geneva 2, Switzerland. Details and an order form will be sent to you by return mail.

Some of the titles to appear recently in the Risk Book Series are:

Konrad Raiser, *To Be the Church: Challenges and Hopes for a New Millennium,* 122pp.

Charles Birch and Lukas Vischer, *Living with the Animals: The Community of God's Creatures,* 96pp.

James B. Martin-Schramm, *Population Perils and the Churches' Response,* 80pp.

David Lochhead, *Shifting Realities: Information Technology and the Church,* 126pp.

Duncan Forrester, *The True Church and Morality: Reflections on Ecclesiology and Ethics,* 104pp.

Eva de Carvalho Chipenda, *The Visitor: An African Woman's Story of Travel and Discovery,* 96pp.

Gillian Paterson, *Love in a Time of AIDS: Women, Health and the Challenge of HIV,* 130pp.